TH

A Com

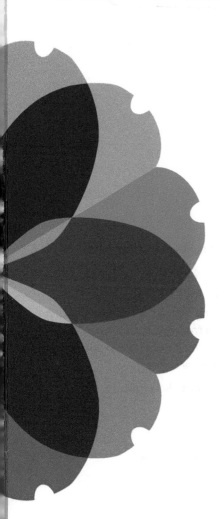

By
Ann Le
Meg Buzzi

Edited by **Isha Aran**
Proofread by **Charlotte Renner**
Book Design by **Elodie Dufroux**
Cover Design by **Shaun Roberts**

Tetra House
www.tetra.house

For the:

Path-finders,
Edge-dwellers,
Wave-makers,
Truth-seekers,
Healers, Helpers, Leaders,
and Teams committed to
Social, Climate, Racial,
Indigenous Justice, and Love.

And all those ready and
waiting for what is to come...

TABLE OF CONTENTS

I. AN INVITATION

THIS BOOK IS AN INVITATION...

to transform how we work.

This is an invitation to pause and observe what is happening around us in this time of great transition. The space between no longer and not yet. An in-between time. A time to cultivate trust, agility, and patience.

The old world, the one that we still exist within, is one of hyper-doing. Our dominant workplace culture evangelizes a hyper-productive, 24/7 "doing" mentality that has convinced us that we exist to do. We sit in meetings from 7-7 only to start in again on email at 10. We are the cliche multitaskers: eating, drafting, managing, driving, and meeting deadlines simultaneously. Finishing the slide deck at 1am. Finalizing the deal while picking up the kids and ordering pizza. We rush to complete the monthly report before that 3-day vacation it has taken us months to schedule, and then we check our email on said vacation.

The culture of hustling, working, doing has defined "success" in this old world. It shows our lives are good and of value, that we are a productive cog in the machine. We've internalized the template for our action-oriented culture: work is virtuous and anything less is a sin.

But it isn't working. And we know it's not working.

Our bodies, minds, and spirits are burned out. Constantly looking to the next meeting, the next deadline, the next contract- has cut us off from ourselves, each other, and the present moment. This chronic doing is unsustainable and harmful, and we cannot continue in the same way we have been.

In this remarkable moment between old and new, a shift is happening. We're seeing an emergent, collective desire of people to be more present to the here and now, to co-create new systems of working that are more sustainable and equitable.

How did we get to this place of feeling so stuck? For some time now, we have been sensing the collective angst. We see the need for new thinking and being with our work and clients. In a spiritual sense, we are in a time of awakening. But how might we invest in our own enlightenment and build new structures to support the ways we want to work together? As we write in the early 2020s, we are seeing colonial and industrial systems crumble and we join a larger call to action to rebuild from a place of equity and love.

How can we stay motivated, and keep our teams motivated in systems that are failing?

The charge of this book is to support you in creating new patterns and thought habits around work and management during this time of transition between the old world and the new one we are all creating. This book will give you space to examine your relationship with work and reimagine what work could mean going forward. It places an emphasis on practices that build the muscle of presence: the art of noticing, quieting our minds, and connecting to our deeper wisdom. Pause, feel, notice.

Take a moment right now to reflect on the following:

What is your work?
What could it ideally be? (Candid leaders, authentic teams, purpose-driven goals...)
What if workplaces and teams supported us as more whole and conscious humans?
What if we showed up as more whole and conscious colleagues?
What if workplaces prioritized relationships?

This book is about asking and reflecting on those questions, growing our individual and collective capacity to achieve fulfillment, work from a place of purpose, and be more aligned as individuals, teams, and organizations.

What exactly is the "in-between?"

We are in it right now. A liminal space where we are watching the world, and therefore the workplace, shift dramatically in real time. The "way we've always done it" is falling apart. At the time of this writing, we're still in the midst of a pandemic, still learning from the historic global protests that shook the world last year, and it seems as though everyday we are faced with a new consequence of climate change. These seemingly cataclysmic cultural and environmental shifts are inextricably linked with how we work.

It's the time of the in-between where, post-lockdown, millions of American workers refused to return to low-wage jobs that offer no benefits. As workplaces tried to reopen, an Ipsos poll[1] reported that over a third of office workers would quit before returning to the office.

The sentiment has changed; priorities re-aligned. According to the global BBMG study in 2020, 6 in 10 people under the age of 30 want the post-pandemic recovery to prioritize "restructuring our economy so it deals better with challenges like inequality and climate change...Young people are looking for a reset rather than a return to the status quo."

70% of Americans hate their job.[2] A WHO study in early 2021 showed conclusively that working over 55 hrs/week led to a dramatically higher risk of stroke and heart disease.[3] Our old way of working is killing us. It's time to begin to "in-source" the care for ourselves that we've been either ignoring or out-sourcing to Netflix binges.

While technology and media continue to accelerate and shape the ways we manage and lead, other social and environmental pressures force us to adapt into work-obsessed people we may not even recognize anymore. Even in this uncertainty, or maybe because of it, the time is ripe for breakthroughs. There is such a need for care, for innovation, for new solutions to old work problems rooted in an unyielding demand for productivity, unrealistic models of success, and the extractive nature of our current economic model.

[1] Mellor, Sophie. "Office workers will quit before going back to the office," *Fortune.* https://fortune.com/2021/07/26/office-workers-to-bosses-quit-if-full-time-back-in-office/. July 26, 2021.
[2] State of the American Workplace Report. Gallup, 2020.
[3] Joint News Release. "Long working hours increasing deaths from heart disease and stroke: WHO, ILO," World Health Organization. https://www.who.int/news/item/17-05-2021-long-working-hours-increasing-deaths-from-heart-disease-and-stroke-who-ilo. May 17, 2021.

The next decade will define how we as humanity support the next few generations. Of course there are fables of doom and gloom, but that's not the whole story. Humanity is challenged to evolve in this moment and yet it is a long-term endeavor. We, as inhabitants of our land and planet, need to upshift and begin to imagine better for all of us.

Our workplaces will not transform overnight and neither will we, but a collective sense of change is here and there is practice to undertake. This work begins with us as individuals. This is an exciting time that asks us to listen deeply, empathize fiercely, and visualize ourselves in a new model of work: a paradigm of self and team leadership that is purposeful, impactful, and led with love.

What can we do right now to prepare for a future we do not know? This in-between time implores us to get creative, urgently. We must write our own grimoires and fill them with the dreams and spells of the way we want it to be. This is critical because the way it is no longer serves us. We are working in a dying system while simultaneously trying to build the next. We are both death doulas and midwives, supporting the old and ushering in the new.

The beauty of our human experience is that we get to be both, and we change and grow through these roles. We have the opportunity to gain wisdom through this challenging time and can be intentional about bringing in the new (as we reimagine work and our relationship to it).

WE'VE BEEN HERE BEFORE
Surfacing wisdom

Staying afloat and continuing to navigate toward our goals (at an individual or organizational level) requires reconnection; to ourselves through reflective practice and with our teams by engaging them in a deeper, more holistic way than we ever have before.

To foster this reconnection amidst these uncertain times, we look to the wisdom of age-old cultural practices alongside the teachings of modern thinkers.

For us (the authors), much of our practice as leaders and changemakers is rooted in wisdom that we have learned from ancient practices of cultures around the world that have been historically cast aside as a result of European colonialism and imperialism.

What are these "ancient practices" and how do they fit in with work? How do we define the ancient? We turn to ancestors, our own respective lineages, and spiritual practices that humans have been creating and observing since long ago. We already see such practices in the workplace: plenty of businesses extol the virtue of mindfulness in the workplace, which has its roots in Buddhist meditation practices. Workplaces these days are all about community building, and what is yogic sangha (the practice of yoga as a group in search of spiritual progress) but just that?

When we talk about surfacing wisdom, we want to honor the ancient, our past, because these tools are not new. In this book's framework, we reference esoteric traditions like shamanism. We define shamanism, for example, as having originated from hunting-and-gathering cultures of long ago. Linked with animism, we will speak of shamanic practices (while they are very complex) as one human being's ability to have a place in the physical world and in the spiritual or transcendent worlds. We honor shamanism as the idea of being truly in-between worlds!

As we become more connected, so does our appreciation for more inclusive ideas and alternate wisdoms. Who knew that so much of that wisdom predates us all? As you study deeper on your own, we hope you will find yourself in awe of how many of these practices, modalities, and systems of studies mirror one another while having originated in their own ancestral tradition around the world.

No matter what your work looks like right now, be it a new project or venture, participating in a team, leading a startup -- you are on this planet at a special time. We are all visionaries in this

moment, nodes in a great network of change. Each of us has the ability to shift, create and heal. For some time now, we've sensed that change is near; some may have called us activists, entrepreneurs, disruptors, but really, what we are is simply "tuned in." More and more, people are activating an intuitive sense about one another, the world, and their place in their life in a way that we haven't seen before. It is this openness, this potential, and this willingness that informs the guiding principles for this book:

- Reframing work as a place for awakening to our potential as humans

- Supporting the building of enlightened, engaged, and fulfilled teams

- Bringing practices of conscious awareness to the workplace; building a conscious organization (note, this isn't "social impact," this is building a collective empowerment by understanding opportunities and challenges in this new age)

- Weaving interdependent work ecosystems: companies, orgs, and non-profits that are committed to a way of being and working together grounded in collective liberation

- Honoring the tools of reflection, work, and wisdom that have been with us for thousands of years

Using our principles and framework we can expand our understanding of self and work, making activities like decision-making more effective. This book presents a series of commitments and practices that invites all parts of yourself into your work. Self-reflection, visioning, and defining agreements are just a few of the ways in which you can create a more integrated and conscious point of view when it comes to team building or daily time management.

Our organizations and our work are ripe with new opportunities to break patterns and gather new information. We want to be really deliberate about shaking up your mental circuitry because we are in that time to re-examine beliefs and those worldviews.

WE WERE MADE FOR THESE TIMES

You've picked up this book because you're ready for this unknown and whatever new world is emerging. As we move into the decade of the 20s, upheavals from the pandemic to protests have forced us to stop what we're doing and take stock of how we got here and why it's not working anymore. None of what has collapsed should be a surprise nor is it an opportunity for sensationalism. We're not here to keep old narratives alive. As truth seekers, we are here for all of it! Serve it up raw and cold and complicated. Whether it's racism, the fall of the patriarchy, or our mistreatment of the environment, we bear witness to the dismantling and we participate in the rebuilding. We are both and between. It's the wake up call of all wake up calls!

THE WHEEL: AN EVER-MOVING FRAMEWORK

The path of discovery is not straight but circuitous; imagine a screw revolving and deepening as it twists into a plank of wood. The cycle of learning keeps us coming back to the things we thought we understood but now access differently. "God is a circle with no circumference whose center is everywhere," described Voltaire. We see this sacred geometry everywhere, and zen masters say that all things in the universe are of one reality, where the principles of no birth and no death and karma operate on a singlesther, clear, and rounded framework. As we process and repeat the phases of the Wheel, the intention is that we begin to see deeper truths with every turn. The Wheel follows old and wise systems that describe and celebrate the numerous transitions that mark our lives. In the framework of the Wheel, we honor liminal phases, too, those that feel in-between. Exactly where we are.

Linear and logarithmic paths have been the historical way to go, right? The most direct and efficient route. "Hockey stick growth," is what the shareholders expect. Birth to death is just a straight line with life in between. We know the dominant patriarchal narrative already. But in this in-between, we have the opportunity and duty to reimagine the narrative to something better. So, how might we get there? And once we are there, how do we know we are 'done?'

We present to you the Wheel, our structure that gives you the opportunity to reflect on yourself, imagine new possibilities for yourself, make those possibilities a reality, and revisit, deepening your understanding of it all.

The Wheel doesn't concern itself with preconceptions you had in the past of attaining all those linear goals we are used to setting for ourselves. Instead of measuring our growth in a straight line or what social media says is 'on brand,' the Wheel keeps turning and gets us deeper with each spin, nudging us into new directions and experiences each time. Imagine a sand anchor, where your continual turning drives your foundation ever deeper. The whole purpose of the Wheel is to keep things moving, and to find yourself moving profoundly with repeating cycles and revisiting and letting go of old stories.

Cultures rich in shamanic practices, honor a spiritual and transcendent life connection, and offer a way for us to see our souls as continual shape- shifters. Whether that's a belief in reincarnation or the ritualistic honoring of a rite of passage (like the Navajo celebration of a baby's first laugh, or the Vietnamese Buddhist fire ceremony to shave a toddler's baby hair, symbolic of past lives, or to acknowledge one's Saturn return in their late 20s). In almost all Shamanic practices, there is an acknowledgement that there is no concept of death. The soul exists in a never ending process of regeneration. Our soul process, like the Wheel, will keep remembering the past, engaging with the present, and preparing for our future selves. The idea here is that we recycle infinitely.

Ancient traditions honor rites of passages of an old way, and not the modern world's marking linear milestones. When we move through a circle, we repeat the cycle of the wheel, not because it's something we need to break, but to honor the endless regeneration that allows us limitless forms and growth. We learn through the process of seeing, reflecting, and experiencing the great mystery of evolution. We're not running around the same circle, but spiraling deeper into wisdom.

HOW TO USE THIS BOOK

This isn't intended to be a linear, read-this-front-to-back-and-you'll-have-it-all-figured-out kind of book. The intention is for you to use the content however it best suits you as a reference guide, as a snapshot of the current moment, as a prompt for discussion in your team, as a tool to help center yourself before a big meeting. This book is a portable support group for your work-weary self.

There are three basic pieces to the book. Part I is our hot take on the present state and how it came to this. Part II describes our framework in detail, using the metaphor of a wheel to describe some simple paths to move through work with more awareness and intention. Part III is less meta and more practical; we invite you to experiment with exercises and activities that bring the Wheel framework into your everyday experience.

For your benefit, we have attempted to curate our most impactful learnings, our observations of work, people, teams, and leadership across a bevy of organizations in our collective years of experience. (You'll hear more about this in Part III.)

Some of these suggestions or exercises (like those that require you to be vulnerable with teammates) can seem counterintuitive at first because we are so used to the capitalist, competitive framing of our workplaces. Much of our conditioning of how we show up to work is rooted in ego. We ask that you give these different modalities a try. Notice and take the time to reflect throughout. See what shows up for you without self-judgment.

ABOUT US

The offerings we've put forth are rooted in our combined 40+ years of experience working across nearly one hundred teams and founders, in our own careers from start-ups, big corporations to nonprofits and academia. We've lived and led in start-up chaos as well as old-school intractable bureaucracy. Most importantly, we ground our real-life experience by calling on the wisdom of practices rooted in history, lineage, and the ancient that we have studied and put to use in our own lives. We've curated these lessons and exercises, adding them to the parts of the Wheel where we saw alignment.

We've been working to drive and support change for a long time. But the modalities, the learnings, the teachings are not new. We've learned from great people, colleagues, elders, and teachers who've learned from others. There is an enormous amount of

past wisdom that remains relevant and timely to our challenges today.

We aren't gurus; we don't want to be followed. What we want to do is PRACTICE and CO-CREATE what truly calls to us. You are your own best guru -- follow your intuition and heart. In surfacing your own wisdom, we have also made our best efforts to provide a diverse acknowledgement of all that has been given to us as humanity. Some of this wisdom arrives from our personal lineages, much does not, but we have studied. We are not experts but wayfinders - We've tried to be explicit about how we've drawn on other cultural wisdom to create this framework. We hope the references serve as the beginning of your own search to delve deeper into so many of the beautiful practices that have come before us.

WHERE ARE WE NOW?

JUST A HEADS UP. WE'RE NEVER GOING BACK.

Whether or not you believe we have arrived at the oft-prophesied "new normal," some things about work have changed permanently, for example a newfound flexibility for those who simply need a laptop and internet to clock in. But some aspects of work haven't changed: low pay, no bennies, long hours.

This lack of radical change where it counts in such revolutionary times can leave us feeling cynical and helpless. Why bother taking ownership of boundaries and reclaiming our authority? Poor management has so often been the culprit of a dysfunctional workplace, that it has become very easy to respond to conflict by simply sending the blame up the chain and denying responsibility for improving our own situation.

We've all been there, we've all taken a moment (ahem, moments) to wallow, but there is an opportunity to empower ourselves to create healthier relationships with ourselves and our colleagues. The real "inner work" still seeks us (Look! You're reading this book right now!), and asks us to examine our contributions to the problem, our blindspots.

"What you seek is seeking you" - *Rumi*

2020 in particular brought us challenges that revealed important connections between our inner work and its relationship to the external world. Systemic racism, inequalities revealed by a global pandemic, a financial system that favors one caste, the brink of climate collapse, and our educational and health systems falling apart are interdependent issues that will take us changing ourselves in order to change the landscape. It has become an active, caring, voice of rebellion to say, I GIVE A FUCK TODAY. It takes a lot of courage, bravery to speak truth to power and CARE. So then, have we finally realized we are all in this together? It was foreshadowed in many ancient cultures that we have arrived at this time of the great Feminine awakening. The Mayan calendar called for this in 2012, astrologers call this the Age of Aquarian order. The Hopi prophesied the demise of humanity around this time if we continued our greed, violence; if we forgot how to honor Mother Earth as our source of life. For those of us who follow the mystic, we've been all surfing the shifts in consciousness.

And for those of you who hear the words "astrology," "energy healing," "Ayahuasca," etc. and say, "Hard pass, no thanks," this book is for you as well, so let's just call this mainstream cultural resurgence of tarot, crystals, past life regressions, and pressed juices as the Age of Kale.

But the past is no longer a prolog. So whether you call this the Age of Aquarius or the Age of the Kale, in this mini epoch, let's agree what is true in the current world sans the woo woo:

- We as humans are losing patience with ourselves and how we exist on this planet;
- Humans are threatening our own existence - through the way we treat each other, animals and nature;
- Today, pandemics, climate crisis, and the uprising against racial and social injustice is driving us to these critical crossroads;
- We are in the process of dismantling many of the systems we've put in place (or that have been placed on us);
- We recognize there is great fear and exhaustion, and those feelings drive our economies, political systems, our religion, our education, our health systems, and how we WORK[4][5]
- It's time to learn to dance in a new way.

We ask ourselves again: **What can we do right now to prepare for a future we do not know?**

---

[4] Rosenbaum, Eric. "What Microsoft found studying work brains in endless meetings," *CNBC*. https://www.cnbc.com/2021/04/20/microsofts-new-outlook-fix-to-end-brain-drain-of-work-meetings.html. April 20, 2021.
[5] Green, Alison. "Office reopening anxiety: Workers are freaked out about going back to their offices," *Slate*. https://slate.com/human-interest/2021/04/office-reopening-anxiety-fear-mistrust.html. April 12, 2021.

THERE IS SO MUCH WAITING TO UNFOLD

This time calls for purging and excavating that which doesn't serve us. There are destructive old habits of our own that have been woven into the very fabric of our society. As products of capitalism, we may have conflated joy with the feeling of "accomplishment." Materialism, false expectations, and celebrity/guru culture may have encouraged us to dumb ourselves down. We may have learned that success means to get followers, to be validated by the crowd. Living inside a hierarchical work system can leave us with the belief that we can never be perfect or enough. Being raised in a growth economy where you are programmed to never just accept what is -- to instead always be striving for better. These inherited beliefs do not serve our ultimate growth or purpose. But as we become aware of them, we have an opportunity to choose a different point of view.

Are you experiencing a calling? A motivation to go deeper? To contribute? For so long the workplace has failed to acknowledge our spiritual selves and needs, the most HUMAN part within us. Our talents, our superpowers. We'll talk a lot about spirituality (and integration). We define these terms here as having a belief that we are connected to something bigger. That there are deep connections between systems. That our ecosystem can also be seen as a collective "oneness." We are all spiritual by nature, we are all "of spirit." It's not about religion, it's about a sense of living in interdependence.

"The old Lakota was wise. He knew that man's heart away from nature, becomes hard; he knew that lack of respect for all living things soon led to lack of respect for humans too."
-Luther Standing Bear

Perspectives rooted in gratitude and presence are key. It doesn't matter the scale or size of your ambition; whether you want to bake a pie for a neighbor or you decide you are going to create a 500+ person global software company. As we look to grow, we look to become a master of ourselves. We seek to be present: to notice and to let go of controlling tension.

In our choices about how we respond to experiences, we invoke spirituality. Only when you know who you are will you have the faith you need to get to where you are going. You are then open to every experience. Gurus, teachers, cult personalities will be unnecessary and out of your way as you make room for your own wisdom.

New rules are forming. It is time to proclaim who you are and what you believe in. Tune into this new radio frequency. Keep breathing and imagining your hopes for your life and this world. We are all guides to bring in deeper change for generations to come.

Astrologically, the Age of Aquarius started December 21, 2020. Collectively, psychologically, and historically it's a once in an 8,000 year shift of time cycle. It's known as the Great Chronocation and it's seismic!

May this book be a chance to honor what was best about the past of your work and to awaken dreams of something better. We meet together in this pursuit, as you are reading these sentences.

Be part of the vanguard to re-create work as the time is presenting itself now. Know that you are not alone.

Seek the growing number of us who hold this dream.

WHAT IS "INNER WORK"

Why do you do what you do? How did you learn what you wanted?

When we refer to inner work, we mean taking radical accountability for our spiritual, emotional, and mental health. This means things like self-reflection, addressing the parts of ourselves that we'd like to improve, understanding our hangups and our needs. Inner work is a process - it's cyclical and it takes a lifetime.

The basis of inner work is a commitment to growth and curiosity, finding the deepest truth you can find in yourself. Inner work includes peeling back the layers of everyone else's ideas of who you should be. It includes choosing which of those ideas you want to keep, and which you want to let go.

Your prototype is never finished.

THINGS WE WILL ENCOUNTER ALONG THE WAY (HOT TOPICS!)

As with any journey of self-reflection and re-creation, using the Wheel will bring up certain themes and ideas that we must grapple with to amplify the work. We've compiled some reflection points, disclaimers, areas to dive deeper, or trigger alerts that we see popping up in the field as we define the new work.

WHY AM I HERE?

We have no idea of the specifics. Not sure if we know our whole purpose here either! You are likely a searcher and a dreamer. From the small fortune we've personally spent on "searching," (admitting the privilege we have to do so) from silent meditation retreats to "mushroom medicine," and guided visioning sessions, we can say we are here to build connection with others and find fulfillment in good work. Every moment in our lives is an experiment. It's time to play and get uncomfortable in service to a new version of ourselves. In feeling the discomfort, you will find the flow in the experiences you are meant to have. We have a choice in each moment to reach for a better-feeling circumstance.

Some of us came into this world with a heavy set of expectations placed upon us. Many of you reading can relate: you don't feel engaged because you were dropped into this nonsense. Or you were sold a bill of goods for how to be, how to act, what your limits are. You became indoctrinated to the feeling of these artificial limits.

But this can shift. It's ultimately up to you to determine your own purpose.

It's fundamentally what the framework and the Wheel is about: we are here to play, disrupt the habits that don't serve us and try new things. You repeat the Wheel and you learn deeper in order to flow. You are here to find your purpose. Every moment and day is intentional.

PRODUCTIVITY

We each have our own personal definitions of productivity (which we've used to judge ourselves and colleagues, developed over years of our own anecdotal observations). Why do we even want to feel productive? Productivity is a buzzword, a goal, a desired state. We want to feel useful. Beliefs like this are largely a modern convention, baked into our culture, affecting our expectations in terms of our own productivity and "worth" in the world. Career trajectories are now about working more than the 8-hour work day, and the constant pressure to value your hours and how much you put forth for survival destroys any semblance of free time.

These are a collage of our cultural, familial, and personal beliefs. For example, our extended families have roots in immigrant stories. The "immigrant work ethic" is a cultural narrative and expectation that was alive in our families and flavored our point of view. This ethic valued hard work, perseverance, and self-discipline. It held productivity and practicality above most things, but the idea that productivity alone should justify anyone's presence in a country isn't the most compassionate approach. Nor is the label realistic; it introduces a fake idea of success that is used to pit minority groups against one another. Rooted in colonialism, it's a false narrative we're also climbing out of.

Let's zoom out for a moment. What is the cost of putting productivity at the center of everything at work? Seeing our success and identity as tied solely to our ability to produce something does us a great disservice. It creates an imbalance by always placing DOING over BEING. Besides the issue of economic fairness, it's a profound proclamation to take back our time from the self-exploitative nature "work" has come to mean. Overemphasizing the "producer" part of ourselves reveals only a fraction of our whole selves, a narrow view of our purpose and contribution. It discounts the value of relationships and dilutes the quality of our offerings in favor of quantity.

Still we want somehow to know that our organizations and teams are effective. How might we reframe our myopic focus on productivity and create healthier team metrics around

quality, effectiveness, and impact? Let's reimagine productivity in more creative terms, taking a very broad interpretation of how our thinking and being together produce generative circumstances with real outcomes. Articulating our (sometimes unconscious) beliefs and noticing or reflecting on what their source might be, helps shed light on how we show up at work.

FAITH

We talk a lot about "spirituality." This doesn't mean prayer breaks in the office kitchen. It doesn't mean religion, but it does have to do with belief.

Spirituality at its most basic is a belief that we are part of something bigger than just our individual selves. It is a recognition that we are part of bigger systems, many of which we cannot see or cannot even comprehend (eg. "the universe"). To be "spiritual" is to access that belief, to look for deeper connections, patterns, or places within and between us. To be spiritual is an acknowledgement that we are more than the sum of our physical, individual parts.

Why is this spiritual perspective important here? Because part of our invitation to work differently together is to notice the connections between our collective struggles and dreams. A spiritual perspective helps us recognize and come back into touch with our whole selves. This combats the negative effects of how current work cultures often encourage us to compartmentalize parts of ourselves and see ourselves as lone wolves in a competitive, corporate landscape.

We tap into a spiritual perspective as we move through this book to allow you to engage in a more holistic and dynamic process of self-reflection than you may have before. To say "spirit," is also to remind ourselves that we are creative souls. The center of our framework, our Wheel, IS SPIRIT. It is the invisible force that connects everyone. The creative juju that allows you and your teams to find flow. And flow tells you you're enjoying the work, allows for unambiguous feedback, proves there is faith in the process.

CAUTION: TRENDY LIGHTWORKERS

Authentic healers and lightworkers do not focus on yoga retreats, flowers, and crystals. You can't be on social media spouting the fluffy parts of a "spiritual walk" and keep the complicated, deep dialogue relegated only to private conversations. A true lightworker will take you through the dark to come to terms with yourself. True healers talk about the ignored and forgotten things, like the collective healing for wounds of the world like racial injustice, economic equality, and environmental collapse. They bring the light where there was none to begin with.

DISCIPLINE/ SELF MANAGEMENT

All the most inspirational ideas, quotes, or posters in the world won't motivate your team if you don't walk the talk. Self-management refers to taking basic responsibility for your behavior and well-being. The discipline piece is about committing to a couple of daily practices that reinvest your energy back into yourself and support that overall well-being. These practices refuel your batteries.

Without them, your impact will be inconsistent; success sporadic. Self-management is about acting as your best self, making choices in line with your values and purpose in the here and now.

We spend our whole careers working on our potential. It's what happens especially in a knowledge worker setting: here's your pay band! Here's the ladder rung! Work hard, you'll get there! Good ol' Protestant (and immigrant) work ethic. There's work to work, and then there's work as a leader to commit and bring integrity and trust to what you say you will do. This is a reminder that your actions must be in service to your dreams.

THE FOUR AGREEMENTS

Don Miguel Ruiz shares the Four Agreements based on Toltec text and practices. Ancient, basic adages that stand the test of time:

1. Be impeccable with your word
2. Don't take anything personally
3. Don't make assumptions
4. Always do your best

ANTAGONISTS

When you read books on leadership or the notion of toxic character traits, they're all quick to reduce the problem to any of the following:

- The Narcissist
- Leader as the false God
- Founder that doesn't trust themselves
- Imposter syndrome / the self-saboteur
- Victim / Martyr/ Bully = triangle of drama
- Leader with no accountability
- Crazy, egoic, but "Visionary" Founder

We've seen them, we've worked with them. But putting "them" into the box of single-issue monikers doesn't quite provide the diagnosis. While the list above are not aspirational traits, striving for the anti-, or canceling them out is also complicated. In life, as we evolve and build, we take on different (maybe not ideal) archetypes in service of the journey of the process.

What is evolution then? What does it take? Fundamentally, it comes down to empathy. For others but also for ourselves. How do we relate? How do we put ourselves in another's shoes? How actively do we listen? Everyone is a leader and a follower at different times of the day. Can we inhabit both roles? When we finally see ourselves as playing different roles, as multi-dimensional beings, we may then understand our connectedness to one another. Taking on a singular identity or "lane" in our lives and in our organization exacerbates

the growing problem we have in communication where we lose our ability to deeply listen. That leads to us having transactional conversations where we are only listening to reply.

PRIVILEGE

Understanding our privilege starts with noticing what we already have. We can't engage with the notion of care without understanding the racial, economic, and cultural dynamics that allow us to access it while prohibiting other folx from accessing it. It's hard to "work on yourself" when you are struggling to meet basic needs or are simply trying to survive. Self-care is for everyone, but certain practices have been staked out and claimed by the privileged.

On top of that, the wellness industrial complex has convinced us that taking care of ourselves is a luxury that more often than not, requires a robust toolbox of expensive instruments and can be exchanged for social currency. Sounds about white.

We don't see our work here together as "white wellness." Instead we are offering resources for you to take a journey of individual, un-selfish care. It is important to acknowledge and reframe conversations around collaboration, practices, and rituals, to be considerate of the privileges of time, resource access, personal identities, and our lived experience. What works for you may or may not work for others. But what is universal is our goal of helping one another to better the collective. When in doubt, choose compassion over advice.

EGO

In leadership (and spirituality), the ego usually gets a bad reputation. There's a lot of focus on the "ego-less leader," or how we need to spend hours in meditation to kick out the evil ego. Ego is often regarded as that selfish, awful thing that keeps you separated from others; the "I." However, we see the ego as a tool, a meaningful compass at times, in navigating our human world. If recognized correctly, it can be seen as a process to how we organize our needs and desires in order to function. When something riles your ego up, take note of why you are responding so strongly, so personally. Instead of "killing the ego," understand it as a protector, something that has been a part of you since you were a child that has helped you cope.

Egos are not the issue, rather, ego-centrism is. Those that are egocentric move through the world as agents for themselves, choosing to stay unaware of the environments around them that influence their lives. A mature and healthy ego allows someone the awareness to see themselves as first and foremost, an agent for the environment, their human community, and then their family, and finally, the self.

For example, you might hear yourself feeling triggered when your need to "win" doesn't manifest. Instead, you can see this as your egoic voice, reminding you that it really is about your need to perform in order to feel worthy of love. Imagine the ego then, as a vigilant soldier, in service to protect. The key is not letting the ego get out of hand; letting that soldier lead you to war each time. When you are in your highest, authentic self, the ego can serve to remind you of your triggers, those feelings of unworthiness, while serving as a voice to remind you to be confident. Let the ego have its place, but remember and acknowledge when it's just your ego speaking.

PROJECTION

Years ago, a senior business analyst became visibly irritated at our team meetings each time the group discussed the work priorities of one of our engineers. "You're not being fair to him," she'd remark in exasperation. "He is overcommitted," she'd say. Each time, the engineer himself sat quietly at the other end of the table, looking awkward.

Our projections shape our reality at work. When we are projecting at work -- we misplace our own feelings onto another. Projection is attributing our own triggers, issues, emotions to a different person or situation. For example, this analyst was likely dealing with her own overwhelm or anxiety when she came to the uninvited 'rescue' of her coworker.

Projection is a big problem in the workplace. When we project, we are foisting our story or baggage onto our peers instead of examining the blind spot that led us to the bad feelings in the first place. The analyst took it upon herself to come to the defense of the engineer, but to what end?

You don't need to defend or go to battle on behalf of another co-worker. Ask instead: What inside me feels tense? What inside me is triggered? What bothers me so much about this dynamic? Slow down and pause. The tension you feel and observe might help you see something you didn't yet see in yourself.

Here are some helpful replacement thoughts to check yourself when you are feeling hot under the collar on behalf of someone else in the office:

"It is not my job to change someone's point of view on behalf of someone else."

"I can be responsible for myself and still care for this coworker."

"I know I am not responsible for anyone else's healing. I want to check the impact of my words/actions on you."

By claiming our own feelings at work we can also release any responsibility we may feel to police the treatment of others or other's feelings. We can relax knowing that we are not responsible for all of our colleagues' circumstances. We can simply hold our own feelings without unnecessarily bearing the weight of other's perceived pain.

WORTHINESS AND SHADOW

For the purposes of the framework, our idea of self-worth is simple. Each person has inherent value. Each of us has unique gifts, voices, and reasons to be here. We are all worthy of fulfillment. We are also part of something larger, greater than the sum of our parts.

Sometimes we become disconnected from these truths, and we may start to question our worth. We may not have a habit of building ourselves up, but rather critiquing ourselves on the daily. How do we build our own self-worth when we catch ourselves in the cliché of being "our own worst enemies?" How we see and judge ourselves can be the most challenging part, right? Your harshest critic stares back at you from the bathroom mirror. When we experience a feeling of low self-worth, we may have lost track of our value, forgotten our purpose.

In an effort to spend more time feeling worthy and connected to self, we recommend a close encounter with your shadow. What do we mean by that? Shadow work is about navigating those parts of yourself that you haven't fully explored or understood yet. The exploration of "shadow" uncovers parts of yourself you may have repressed or are not yet comfortable surfacing. (For example, you may not realize that the reason you hate to hear your manager yelling is because he sounds like your father did when you were a kid.)

Shadow is what you are feeling at your core, way beneath the actual thing you are experiencing at the surface. You feel that sore spot? But what created it? When you are hurt, there is something unresolved that requires your attention and "doing the work" can also be with a professional (Coaches, therapists, healers -- they are all critical to how we process and grow, and we urge everyone to get curious about personal growth). It needn't be alone. If you don't ask for what you need, that need will keep getting bigger.

For some, it helps to take the perspective that we as human beings are called to serve. It is not about seeing yourself or others as worthy or unworthy, in so much as it's about accepting a point of view of service to others and to the planet, to the bigger game. Accept this divine duty and you will no longer question whether or not you are worthy. No one but YOU can fulfill your purpose!

GROWTH MINDSET

Do you often view situations as problems to be solved or avoided altogether? Does an unexpected twist at work usually seem like an opportunity? Do you get excited to tackle challenges? Or perhaps it feels tiring just thinking about it.

The psychologist Carol Dweck tells us, "growth mindset is based on the belief that your basic qualities are things you can cultivate through your efforts...Everyone can change and grow through application and experience...The passion for stretching yourself and sticking to it even (or especially) when it's not going well, is the hallmark of the growth mindset."

Our old world over-valued the "expert" mindset: a certain pedigree defined only by a degree, a resume at face value, longevity in a position, only your "past" counts. It assumes that talent and abilities are fixed. While these attributes do go far, it does not reward the value of professional development and growth both personally and in a team nor the fact that abilities can be developed with effort.

Developing a growth mindset over an expert one is critical because it centers persistence and commitment toward our purpose or goal. A growth mindset invites us to see obstacles as opportunities to innovate or adapt, bumps in the road become re-framed as a chance to grow, pivot, and evolve.

Dweck articulates the central reason behind the importance of having a growth mindset: actively cultivating a perspective of growth helps us to flourish even in difficult circumstances. Adopting this way of seeing the world can assist us in adapting to the shifting workplace we are experiencing right now.

OLD STORIES

Acknowledging our old stories is key to moving forward. We each have legitimate wounds from our past, and we get to decide how long we suffer with them. Through this process, we ask you to reflect on old stories. Are there some that no longer serve you? What might be possible if you detached from some of those narratives?

Rather than spending your energy worrying or re-living what happened back then, invest that same energy in developing your agility. Agility in this context means the daily practice of noticing when you are in an old story, and then allowing yourself to choose something different. Developing these gifts improves your ability to deal with uncertainty and be able to reframe past wrongs into new opportunities.

The path to self-awareness is not an easy one -- you have to choose what you want to improve as well as choosing to free yourself from the stories you love to tell. While you may find yourself in cycles of dysfunction, past pain is not a predictor of the future. It must be acknowledged, processed, and reconciled or otherwise let go.

Find your community; this journey doesn't have to be solo. Notice the stories you share. Our stories are a reflection of our worldview, how we present our energy to the outside. People respond to the energy we wear and the stories we inhabit. By creating new stories for ourselves, we can create better and more fulfilling futures with the people who share our aims.

THE ANCIENTS WERE TALKING ABOUT NOW!
The start of the "Aquarian" age in Hellenistic astrology coincides with the dawn of Toltec new sun or "Sixth Sun" that occurred in 2020. According to Mesoamerican culture, the "Fifth Sun" (represented by Tonatiuh), was a warlike and fierce God who began to lose his strength toward the end of Mayan Calendar. The Fifth Sun represented an era where humanity engaged in domination of one another. The reign of the Sixth Sun was to herald a return to nature and to the wisdom of the natural world. Translated as "inside of the Sun" this new era also calls us to explore internally our own consciousness. It also embraces a refreshed concern for the collective!
(Aztec prophecy of Cuauhtemoc 1521)

SLOWING DOWN (TO MOVE FAST)

Slowing down is scary because our daily lives are built around things like measuring our productivity, multitasking, instant gratification, to-do lists, etc. Slowing down could allow the past to catch up with us! When you slow down, things become quiet. It's scary because the quiet has become so rare, so uncommon. We have lost touch with the quiet. In quiet, you start to notice feelings. You begin to feel because your emotions have a slower pace than your mind. When you slow down even more, then your body, too, can catch up because the pace of the body is even slower than your emotions.

Through the slowing down of the pace of your life, things emerge from our past that are not yet digested, that have not yet been integrated.

It is natural to feel moments of darkness when you are regularly "in the work" of reflecting. It can be uncomfortable to excavate or even to ask yourself some of these questions. For example, you may recognize something about yourself that you feel suddenly desperate to change. You may want to hide with embarrassment from some of the insights that come up. In reflection, you are seeking a truth inside yourself. It becomes a place where you can begin to separate the thoughts that belong to your ego, and the thoughts from your soul, authentic self.

In the midst of exhuming this truth, it can be challenging to be shown to yourself. But there is a great opportunity here to re-frame these feelings that arise as insight and information rather than shadow and fear. When these kinds of thoughts or feelings arise, you can take a deep breath, pause, and regard this information with compassion. Stay courageous and keep coming back to the practice of reflection, however you design it. Allow the process of reflection to unfold and prepare you for deeper learning.

YOUR BODY AND THE PHYSICAL ENVIRONMENT

In our go, go, go culture, our physical bodies and spaces can be neglected. The scenes are familiar: back to back meetings without breaks, falling asleep with our phones during a meal, 10+ hours hunched over a laptop... Now more than ever these cumulative habits are manifesting as challenges, injuries, and illnesses. It sounds basic, but stretching, drinking water, and clearing your lungs with fresh air can clear stale energy and re-ground your body. Decluttering and cleaning your spaces serve as an important spiritual cleansing as well.

As more and more of the world moves to remote work, and folx set their own schedules in the gig economy, there is a greater opportunity to pay attention to your surroundings and how you move through space. Here are a few mini embodiment routines to get you back to yourself:

Incorporate sound.
Sing out loud, play music, bang a pot and spoon! Reset the energy in your workspace or knock yourself out of a stale mood.

Go barefoot for a walk outdoors.
A quick 5 minute stretch outside will serve as an important pause as you work through the Wheel. If you can, spend a moment barefoot on the soil, sand, or grass. Take a moment for a deep breath, and consider the connection of your feet on the planet.

Clear a space.
Consider cleaning as a ritual. Notice what you've outgrown, honor the

45.

past and give yourself healthy space for the new. Consider incorporating a meditation area as part of your new environment.

BOUNDARY ISSUES

Everyone talks about them. It's in your horoscope to "work on them." They're now a part of corporate mission statements, in your memes, your social media, and are also co-opted by that coworker as an excuse to cut and run from accountability. They rarely involve actual maps.

Boundary issues are often temporary or longer-term entanglements or enmeshment with another person, place, thing, mineral, or vegetable. (Usually parents, let's be honest.) Boundary issues can present themselves at work when you can't say No to your teammate's request, or when your boss asks for unpaid weekend time. Boundaries exist, and like the south node of Mercury when Taurus is rising will always highlight, they are something you are usually "working on."

Here's where boundary issues may come up with your work in the Wheel. We

support interdependencies (if that's what you desire to build), but we want you to be clear about codependency and what it means to create together. Boundary issues bleed into our inability to have independent relationships. Get clear on where someone else ends and where you begin.

Otherwise, it will muddle the sense of who you are when you're enmeshed with another. If you can remember that you are whole and magnetic, and you remember you are exactly where you need to be, it helps the feeling of that entanglement to now dissipate.

ESTHER HICKS SUMMARIZES THROUGH THE *LAW OF ATTRACTION*.

When it comes to excessive worry or seeing someone in only a place of suffering:

- It is not your responsibility to feather someone's nest, nor is it theirs to do the same for you
- It is not possible for you to control the conditions someone has created around them
- If you expect others, or want to provide others, to give you the perfect conditions to thrive, then you would be giving up your power to create your own experiences.

The takeaway - choose to see your loved one in a place that is thriving. No one needs your pity.

THE TRAP OF THE INTELLECT

Modern society has come to overvalue the intellect, we've prioritized analyzing, finding evidence, and relying on prior information in order to make decisions and make our case to one another. Humanity's intellectual advancement is why we are where we are today. But we've come to value only the "intellectual thought process" and have not led with our heart, emotion, or intuition. We've come to revere the intellect to the exclusion of the heart connection. Spiritual master Sadhguru calls "the intellect" an instrument that we should only use "to dissect and know things." Intellect is an important tool; like a knife, it analyses, slices and dices, and breaks down problems and situations. But the intellectual "tool" is overused. Would you use a tool like a knife to build a team, or stitch together a loving relationship, or create an open and happy company culture?

The natural way to be is to experience life with our intellect AND our heart and our spirit -- together! An integrated, intellectual and spiritual human. What meditation and slowing down allows us to do is to set aside that important tool we call a brain, and instead listen to and honor our HEART intelligence. Our modern culture has forgotten the heart. By remembering it through meditation you can renew your relationship to your intuition and other ways of knowing. Meditation isn't about stopping your mind. It allows you space to set down your brain and to see what other intelligences you can use to move from experience to moment.

GRATITUDE

Yes, gratitude! Yes thank yous, thanks-givings and friends-givings. All the yeses, and the appreciation of all-the-little-things. (Even gratitude for the gratitude journals that seem to infiltrate too many conversations over brunch- the lists that may sound like an exercise for the privileged.); for those who didn't have the experience of housing insecurity or a cancer diagnosis to put a damper on "what I'm super thankful for today."

Gratitude is core to spirituality and early belief systems. Buddhism speaks to gratitude as a way to experience yourself as more present, more full and here than ever before. Dating as far back as ancient Sumer (3,00 BC), the act of creating gratitude lists has long been a part of pagan and wicca religions, especially during Lammas (Harvest Celebration) and Mabon (Autumn Equinox) holiday honoring harvest and the bounty of nature. Putting pen to paper in the form of expressing gratitude is powerful. But what it really opens us up to is helping identify and tap into our value systems. Writing down what we are grateful for and taking that moment to express and meditate on that, tells us something about what we value and ultimately helps us understand who we are. Gratitude is also about seeing ourselves within humanity and the ways we are always able to catch one another and see the others' needs.

Gratitude can be strange when it exists in conflict with our desire for more: more time, wealth, love, abundance. But gratitude allows us to shift our frequency. Things are down, we're a little depressed, but what are we grateful for at this very moment? And in our expression of gratitude, we can also ask, what are we going to bring into our lives in this in-between?

We begin to notice a more expansive point of view. Gratitude allows you to see a bigger version of yourself. What we are grateful for means we've picked through and identified the experiences that nourish us; to fully comprehend the scope of our prosperity.

And yet, some of us may find writing down our blessings a very difficult thing to do. Are there activities you may take for granted? Access to healthy food, an easy commute to work, or the ability to have a clean space. Sometimes, seeing your prosperity can also bring about some guilt, but know that you are just opening your heart to further gratitude and compassion when feeling this, too and seeing the grace around us.

BUDDHISM'S FOUR NOBLE TRUTHS
Human life has a lot of suffering.
The cause of suffering is greed.
There is an end to suffering.
The way to end suffering is to follow the Middle Path.

GRIEF

There's a PBS kids show called Daniel the Tiger, a favorite episode (with its own catchy jingle) announces, "Sometimes you feel two feelings at the same time." Their conclusion? "That's OK!" Life contains a full variety of experience. Light and dark, yin and yang. It is possible to feel gratitude and grief in the same breath. Grief and change go hand in hand. You can honor grief and allow it to co-exist with gratitude. Let yourself feel it all.

Loss is one of the most painful experiences we as humans go through. We honor grief and traditionally provide space for the sorrow of losing a parent, a family member, a relationship, a career or pet. But the grief we are pointing to here is the kind we experience as we let go of an old version of ourselves or our work. At these times of becoming a new you, you lean into new dreams and mourn the old stories you must let go of in service to the new. The old must dissolve to make way. That can hurt. The new you might disrupt the old way you earned a living, or talked to your parents.

Within the experience of grief, there are moments where we intellectually understand the process we are in, but our emotions are in a different place altogether. You may be surprised by what comes up or the way it lands. We may find ourselves feeling so full and energized for what's to come, but ragged, flattened or heartbroken a moment later while pondering what is still imperfect or unfinished.

INTEGRATION

Integration is about creating wholeness. There are pieces of ourselves that are hidden even to ourselves. These are beliefs or attitudes or feelings or assumptions of which we remain unconscious. What else is down inside there? Who else might you be underneath the layers and intersecting parts? When you notice you are angry or irritated yet cannot for the life of you figure out why you feel that way, it can sometimes be an indicator of a hidden aspect of yourself you have yet to uncover.

Reflection is the practice of investigating these parts. As they surface, you can begin to unknot them and glean knowledge about yourself. You process and absorb these parts, you decide what belongs to you, what you want to keep and what no longer serves you.

While some part of us looks forward and believes that peace and grace will come, another part inside of us acknowledges that it doesn't feel that way now. It feels stuck or dark. Grief requires time for us to heal mentally, emotionally, physically, spiritually. Our work is to integrate all of those ways of knowing and feeling back together. Sitting, praying, meditating or other practices of grounding can help you focus on your inner peace in order to seed and grow what's next.

The complexity of our work environments demand that we show up more fully as ourselves. How else can we make conscious and wise decisions for ourselves, our teams and our families if we are only in touch with fragments of ourselves?

What does your team know about you? For many of us, our daily hours are consumed interacting with our coworkers. Yet there are parts of your personality, your passions, your interests, your backstory, that are hidden from the very people you spend 40+ hours a week on Slack with. What understanding might they gain if they knew more about who you truly are?

WHAT YOU THINK IS WHAT YOU GET

We're here to call for big, outrageous, glorious change. We don't have to know how it will come into our life, but the Wheel can help lay the groundwork for its arrival. If we are on autopilot all the time, distracted by the general noise of a given day, we might miss the signs of a bigger shift. The journey here is to cultivate a regular practice of being present and noticing. The more we pause, the more we take a moment to slow down and take stock of our distractions, the more we are able to come off of autopilot and truly be intentional and to be in touch with what we want.

The law of attraction sounds simple (aka "like attracts like," manifesting, cognitive reframing), yet it is a journey to shift our thought habits toward imagining and leaning into how we'd like our lives to feel. With our thoughts, we create the circumstances our mind dwells upon -- positive or negative.

The phases of the Wheel are reminders to refocus on who you want to be in the world. This includes spending time in quiet thought, recalibrating the frequency of your desires, and pushing your energy to the goal(s) of your creation. You also will prepare for the arrival of the dream on every level: material, physical and spiritual. You don't know how it will come but you must trust that it will.

SELF-CARE

When a boss tells an exhausted employee to take a yoga class or get their nails done, that is not self-care. A spa day is not going to bring self-empowerment. We are going to offer a definition of self-care that may be slightly different from what the yogurt commercials might lead you to believe.

The notion of self-care is bandied about like a fleeting luxury, like some secret excuse to nap. Self-care gets a bad rap, because along with "wellness," it places the responsibility for the fix (as well as the blame) on the individual who is burned out to begin with. We would argue that our broken system of work, among other things, bears great responsibility for blurring our work/self boundaries.

Let's start by recognizing that we all have limits. Self-care can be a practice of saying no, stating your boundaries, and no longer participating by playing the martyr. We're not talking about Joan of Arc here. We're talking about the ways in which we push ourselves to the limit in order to fulfill someone else's expectations. Our current culture has a tendency to praise pain and suffering in the name of the greater good. Stay the extra hour, take that extra meeting. But sacrifice does not guarantee acknowledgement, attention, or sympathy.

As a leader and advocate, you have the chance to be a vocal part of your organization and your team to advocate against burnout and the harms we do to ourselves when we tie our self-worth to our culture of toxic, relentless productivity.

Here are some helpful tips around boundary-setting as a form of "self-care:"

- Release the idea that it's cool to be busy and efficient.
- Say NO. To obligations, to holding space without permission, to holding other people's trauma. And understand that it's YOU that needs to say no, not someone else.
- Acknowledge you have limits; what are they?
- Let go of martyrdom and victimhood. Can't "self-care" when you're dead.
- Do not feel bad for setting boundaries; know instead that it is an act of empowerment.

Check out the Native Wellness Institute, an organization expressly devoted to the well-being of indigenous people; they've created research and important models that reach for modalities of happiness. We prefer to focus on what makes you thrive and flow, rather than lean on self-care only when shit gets tragic and dark.

55.

COLLECTIVE CARE

While scrolling through your social media feeds, the idea of self-care is sandwiched between the hard news and your friends' virtue signaling. While it is crucially important to replenish ourselves, the ways in which we replenish, and the sources we turn to for care, are worth examining. Beyond the bath salts and infrared massagers, we also need community care.

Community care is about noticing and serving our collective needs and honoring that we are all in this together. Individualism is over and interdependence is (back) in. Examining the boundaries between self and team or self and community helps us uncover what it is we really want in service of the collective or trying to figure out how we create the future we all desire and deserve. The reflection exercises we present in our framework (see Part III) are in service of examining your life more deeply and holistically.

To do this, we must look beyond the usual self-help or self-care trends which, rather than asking for radical reflection of the obsolete systems we live in, often ask us to change to better suit the systems. We talk the talk, and speak with vigor from self-help books from successful Silicon Valley types. "Lean in," they say; use OKRs to mitigate those risks;

speak like that guy (and it is usually a guy) to inspire others. So many of these ideologies we usurp and twist to pretend they are our own strong opinions when they are little more than ad campaigns we can step away from. Instead, we must demand thought leadership that promotes and expands systems of collective care and prosperity.

Today, the seismic change occurring in our world might seem like an unraveling of everything we knew before. During this in-between, we get the chance to reexamine our lives, and play the designers of what we want our world to be.

Have we asked ourselves: What does it feel like when I am out of balance? In balance?
What do I need to thrive?
What is my highest hope for this culture?
Where do we want to put our focus and effort?

This is a re-grounding of ourselves to the present moment and what we yearn for in our home and work-lives. The solutions to the pressures we feel are internal rather than external. Yes, we are trained to look outward- taught, for example, that gadgets and data (think: fitbits and other wearable tech) are the answer to our lives. That tracking our stress will alleviate our stress. Whether that's true or not, relief is available inside you without a single product or guru.

What would it look like for real change, where work isn't about productivity milestones, but includes rest, balance, and harmony? If our government and corporate leadership doesn't offer us change, we must declare it, inspire it, and demand it.

The Vedic Life: The Four Ashramas

The Ashramas are one facet of Dharma in Hinduism, first mentioned in medieval Indian texts. Rather than #lifegoals, the concept simply provided a framework for fulfillment, happiness, and spiritual liberation.

1. Brahmacharya (student life) - Young, free, student, learning and apprenticeship
2. Grihastha (household or family life) - Pair up, make some kids
3. Vanaprastha (retired life) - Bye kids, bye job, giving back; literally the "forest dweller"
4. Sannyasa (renunciation) - Letting go of worldly things

While we've separated from these "job goals" in contemporary life, in the framework of the Wheel, we honor self-reflection and the parts that lead to spiritual emancipation. Especially the part about wandering the forest, which sounds pretty nice.

PRESENCE AND PATIENCE

I can't leave my phone or my laptop. Never have a minute to myself. I'm a parent juggling my overloaded work, growing children and a partner. I haven't showered in two days. How do I get grounded and back in touch with myself?

Being "present" isn't about hardcore silent retreats or meditating for hours until you levitate. To become more patient with yourself and connect to a better-feeling energy, sit and slow down. Practicing sitting and slowing prepares us for active change by connecting us to what is going on in the here and now. But before you dive into the planning, the execution and the harvest, we have to feel the now. Be here now. And in this present moment, we pause to make sure things are fluffed and folded before we move on.

Going through the motions of life, dwelling on should-haves and supposed-to's won't give you the silence you need to imagine what you are going to bring forth into your life and the world. Being present is also about paying attention. The core of the reflection phase of the Wheel is about slowing down to see the roots of your being, to be more present moment to moment. It is time to notice the story you carry deep inside you, in your soul. Some of that story needs to be released, and some of the story will highlight the abundance of resources inside yourself.

59.

While current wisdom says it takes 28 days to form a habit, committing to 5 min/day for a week is often enough to provide some relief and clarity to your busy mind. Start small, and we believe you will get hungry for more, you will begin to claim even more quiet space for yourself. And in that space, you will feel better. In that space, you will make discoveries.

Be here now. In our busy lives (online or IRL) it is important to manage distractions if we want to fulfill our purpose. We'll talk a lot about meditation, stillness, listening to intuition, and will offer some examples of those practices. What is the deal with getting to the now? Even in its simplicity, stillness is what allows you to quiet down, slow down and prevent you from making decisions in haste. It helps sharpen your focus. Meditation or practicing mindfulness provides space to connect with your intuition, to see the flow, and helps you

move forward wisely. Put away all of the distractions and sit with just yourself in this exact moment right now. You, your breath, this moment. That is all there is.

SETTING INTENTIONS

Setting your intention is not the same thing as making goals. Zen Buddhism teaches us that intention is not oriented around a future outcome. The practice of intention is a focus on "being" in the present moment. Goals are associated with finding a place in the world and feeling effective; intention provides unity and connectedness in your life. Intention isn't always a feeling like "I intend to have this difficult conversation with grace," it is also intentioning for the very best outcomes that you put your heart and soul in.

Try less multi-tasking where you are doing one thing and thinking of something else. Multi-tasking is necessary at times, but try balancing it with intentional work, too. Get intentional with the coffee-making ("I intend for this coffee to wake me up in the best way"), give your full intention to doing the dishes without any distractions ("I love these dishes, they hold my food and I wash them with care"). Owning these actions will help you feel alive in your bodies.

IMAGINATION

Our imaginations are the primary engine for our dreams. They inform our interests and fund our curiosity. Somehow as we grow older and spend more time in the work world, we lose some of our connection to the wild imagination we had in our youth.

But we are here to tell you that you can reclaim that magical thinking, and you MUST (!!!) to thrive in this in between. Imagination is a crack of light breaking through the ordinary. It's the spark of a delicious feeling. It's a chance and a hope. Imagination is a gateway to possibility. And possibility is what we all need more of in our current world: for ourselves, our workplaces, the climate. So each of us needs to do her part in waking up this aspect of ourselves as a means to finding novel ways to make our lives feel better at the micro and the macro levels. Most of us need a refresher to get our imagination muscles back

in working order. Allow yourself to DAYDREAM. Set a timer for 15 minutes. Sit back, close your eyes and wander. Our imaginations might require some "ground-breaking," some softening of the outline of who we think we are everyday. We are cracking the shell of the practical adult person on the outside and getting to our core -- coming back to who we are (and always were).

II. LIKE A WHEEL: FOUR PHASES

HOW TO BEGIN

It's easy to feel cynical about changing our work habits during this period of upheaval. DOES ANY OF THIS MATTER given that systems and institutions are in the midst of DISMANTLING? Is everything broken beyond repair? Shouldn't we wait for the walls to come down before we start imagining how to build the new rooms?

Let's take a breath. We know many of the ways we function as a species are in need of an upshift. Most of our systems require big fixes and adaptation (e.g., healthcare, food, education, transportation, etc.) Some of the foundations of these systems were never solid to begin with! So too, our internal systems and ways of working, being, and creating must evolve. While big changes are happening in the world writ large, our interior conditions shift too. As within, so without.

Sometimes this feels dramatic and other times gradual or subtle. When have you felt this kind of movement, these shifts? In creating this framework, the Wheel, we've taken into consideration the challenges above and recognize that there are varying layers to the shake up. With the help of many ancient wisdoms, we invite you to reflect and elevate: shake out the low frequencies, the old habits, the snark. Imagine getting a deep clean, an internal brillo pad, as we clear out what will not take us into the future.

As we introduce you to the Wheel, it asks us to embrace ourselves as agents of change. Each one of us is a vector for new ways and ideas out in the world and within ourselves. To become innovators for something better, we begin by slowing down and noticing the old habits and patterns within us. This is the beginning of a more conscious and connected time.

Crisis precedes transformation. The night is darkest before the dawn, as the cliché goes. There will be mountains to climb and valleys to reflect in as we journey toward more conscious ways of working and being. What do our future leaders, including us, need in a time of great change? When we ask: How will we live now? What feels like a true answer?

This is how we began thinking about the Wheel.

Where does the practice of the new begin?

Personally.
It can start with showing up differently to work; deciding to be more conscious about how we participate and lead. That means connecting to and bringing our whole selves, consciously, into the workplace. (We already do this, just not consciously.) This journey will change our predominant narrative around work, so we can begin leading from our wholeness. It means authenticity, vulnerability, and candor in what we do, say, and be at work.

When we talk about energy it's about noticing how our feelings affect how we show up. Low frequency feels dense, heavy. (Ever have moments stuck with an energy vampire? Or a "venting" session that was really just gossip, complaining and playing the victim?) The feeling of physical exhaustion from a conversation, the mental fog. When we vibrate "high," it's no different than showing up as our highest positive version of ourselves. It's not asking you to turn away from reality, it's just getting out and ahead of what doesn't work. We emanate a personal power, peace and clarity and joy in all we do. Vibrate high, and there's little room for pain or discomfort.

Ancient symbolism found in the Dharma Wheel and Mandala (of Hindu, Buddhist, Jain, and Shinto beliefs), the Medicine Wheel of multiple indigenous North American cultures, and the pagan Witch's Wheel reminds us that all movements are ever changing. So it's purposeful that we've envisioned this framework as a wheel, in which there is no beginning and no end. The Wheel is always moving, beginning, and ending in turn.

This Wheel is here to guide us through the In-Between. We invite a circular practice to support both a personal awakening and practical upgrade for a team's work strategy. One of our goals in writing this book was to make space to practice asking powerful questions and reflecting on our experiences. Perhaps the Wheel will serve as a tiny piece of our larger learning, or it may become something more significant. Just by picking up and reading this book, you are already part of experiencing and investing in the upshift each of us needs.

THE FIRST TURN

THE FOUR PHASES

The Wheel consists of four phases: Reflect, Design, Enact, and Allow. Each phase has a distinct vibe, a flavor. Each contains an invitation to expand your point of view. You may spend a differing amount of time or energy in each phase. Some work may feel more comfortable and easy than other work. You may feel more committed to the work of one phase over another. Great! There is no set expectation around how long you might choose to explore the questions of one particular phase or exercise, or where you want to start. What we will mention is that western culture favors action over inaction, doing over being. The phases of the Wheel that focus on presence and pause (Reflect and Allow) might be a place to spend more time in general, as they represent a learning edge for many of us.

What's most important is that you begin wherever your curiosity feels most alive. As a change agent for a new way of working, consider your own needs first. You have the ultimate agency to determine where you want to explore. Choose your own adventure!

THE PHASES:

Reflect - Mindfulness, preparation and grounding. This is about noticing. Slowing down. An examination of core values, and your personal point of view. It articulates the purpose and connects us to the present situation.

Design - Intention-setting, organization, whiteboarding and ideation. This is about assembling the idea. Put pen to paper and begin the blueprint of the desired outcome, experience or future state.

Enact - Action, execution, initiation. Building the team and materializing the idea. This is where your blueprint comes to realization. This is the making-shit-happen, Superheroes-come-together-and-kick-butt-as-a-team portion of the Wheel.

Allow - Letting go, letting what needs to emerge, bringing forth acceptance, breathing room. Allow = Trust. This is about pausing and getting some air. The ship has been built, allow it to set sail and see where it goes. The work is letting go while not allowing self-doubt to creep in.

There is no beginning or end to the cycle per se. Its circuitous nature has us re-visiting each place again and again, while growing deeper in our learning. While later we'll be able to drop in at different phases, the sequence will remain the same. Rinse and repeat.

ALLOW

REFLECT

ENACT

DESIGN

> *"A leader is best when people barely know he exists; when his work is done, his aim fulfilled, they will say: we did it ourselves."* -Lao Tzu, 605-531 B.C.

ARCHETYPES ON THE WHEEL

An archetype is a character or symbol that evokes a universal emotion or milestone that carries across the human experience. The Hero, the Fool, the Lover, these are all archetypes, as are the benevolent Queen or the Best Friend. They are malleable, but the core idea is that these embodied symbols give us the ability to recognize a variety of aspects of ourselves and our lived experience quickly and deeply. Archetypes can help us call in our best selves, project outward, and practice being who we most want to be.

Here on the Wheel, we offer an archetype that characterizes or exemplifies each phase. Think of it as a suggested role or point of view to try on at each of these phases. Each role challenges us to stretch our comfortable usual perspective, to visit new territory. What feels unfamiliar to one of you in one part of the Wheel might feel like a happily typical place for another reader. We don't want to pigeon-hole you, we just want you to try on these hats and notice what feels tight, what feels unusual, what feels easy, what feels like a stretch, or even scary. As you experiment with adopting or connecting to these personas, we encourage you to choose a beginner or growth mindset. While one of these roles might fit like a glove, we encourage you to spend time outside your usual comfortable place.

VISIONARY (Reflect) - In a world of infinite possibilities, the visionary uses meditation, reflective time, and contemplation to be out of the thinker mode. They see the potential of everything, removes the noise to listen, discern,   and rest. Knows that life is only limited by the boundaries of our own beliefs. When the guardrails come down, how will we investigate what's been growing at the edges and what might become the future dream?

INVENTOR (Design) - The Inventor is both artist and pragmatist. While we've taken off the visionary hat, this is still in a place of creative self-expression now applied to the right-aligned work we love in order to articulate and bring the vision to life. Be analytical, stay thoughtful. As an outcome, the Inventor lays out a roadmap to accomplish the vision.

CONDUCTOR (Enact) - As the leader of the orchestra, the conductor is the executor of the masterpiece. They know all the instruments and direct when and where others need to come to the fore or to take a back seat. While the work is in execution, a conductor is often also a teacher, a conduit. How will we now direct, guide and execute on the vision and roadmap?

STEWARD (Allow) - The steward holds the whole system as work is getting done. How might we serve and protect the collective vision? To do so means to be in a place of TRUST and allow for the work we've done to be on its journey. You allow the Universe, self and others to do what needs to happen.

BASIC PRACTICES FOR THE WHEEL

THE SPIN

The Wheel is applicable in a myriad of arenas, whether it's vetting a business plan to make sure it showcases total dedication of thought and resources, to addressing a specific problem on a project. It can also serve the personal, guiding you through questions like, "What do I want to be when I grow up?" Eventually, as the quadrants become familiar, they help us notice and consider more nuanced problems like, Why are we in an enact phase when we haven't even thought through the design? For teams, the Wheel can serve as important shared nomenclature, for project discussions or team communications or even how you show up personally in your relationships.

Each of the Four Phases of the Wheel includes:

· A detailed introduction about the Phase
· Archetype and leadership values to explore
· Practices and experiments to try
· When to move on to the next Phase

When it comes time to decide on cycling again through the Wheel, there is no right or wrong. Like a medicine wheel, use the framework to cement your philosophies and beliefs, and offer your prayers and intentions. The Wheel reflects your strengths and weaknesses back to you, showing you what you may need to learn again and again. Life is a circle and what goes around comes around. Learn from every iteration as you move forward.

In Part III, templates and reflection exercises provide further details to help structure this important work.

More on the Medicine Wheel. The oldest Medicine Wheel goes back 5,000 years and was found in Majorville, Canada. More than 70 sacred hoops can be found in North America alone. While each wheel is unique, they all represent and tell the story of the first people emerging as Spirits from the underworld. It can be seen as a transcendent map that represents your life; a circle of awareness.

CREATING SPACE FOR YOURSELF

1. Start now by doing one thing at a time, try the "smallest next indicated thing" (SNIT) or the "minimum viable experiment" (This could be as simple as making your bed if you're feeling like the whole day is a loss! Or it could mean the roughest draft of one paragraph you need to write for a work report). The key is to make it doable and tiny!
2. Devote time daily to meditation, sitting, or other quiet contemplation (this is critical)
3. Put space and pauses between things; beware the multi-tasking - SLOW DOWN
4. Carve out time to develop, create, or discover rituals and habits that restore
5. Do less; think about what is actually necessary
6. Balance action with just BE-ing
7. Stay mindful of your capacity; notice if you have a tendency to accelerate
8. Move to release stress and feelings held in the body
9. Take breaks; it doesn't all have to happen at once
10. Find a culturally competent facilitator, therapist, coach or healer to support this work

CO-CREATING SAFETY IN YOUR TEAM

1. Listening deeply (This is the simplest, most effective, and often most difficult skill.)
2. Acknowledge one another; is everyone seen, heard explicitly?
3. Practicing appreciation to each other, starting with gratitude and respect
4. Having our feelings, thoughts, and experiences mirrored back and validated
5. Sharing collective space; giving one another permission to show up as our whole selves

TIME IS CIRCULAR

Spend as much or as little time as you need to sit and "be here now" for whatever phase you are in. Part of the work is a personal journey, regardless of whether you are working on the Wheel alone or with a team. An operations manager may find that they are breezing through the ENACT phase, while maybe needing more time in REFLECT. An artist might find the ALLOW phase to be something they can move through quickly while DESIGN is the hardest because they fall prey to perfectionism in the details. Perhaps you enjoy novelty and surprise, but other phases feel difficult because you are unwinding an old habit of doing and thinking about these things. Some areas will need more cleaning out than others; some more consideration of whether or not their sparks are sparks of joy.

Notice: What feels easy along the way? What feels scary along the way? Make a note of it.

What matters is the continuing practice of reflection. Cultivating an ability to stop, sit, listen in the present. You can't jump into the next until you experience the NOW. In the same way you must secure your own mask before helping others, you must slow down and reflect before moving on.

The Bardo is known as the "intermediate state." The term comes from what is known in the West as the Tibetan Book of the Dead, which considers 'death' merely a state of transformation. In the Bardo, we process the change. We transform. The Bardo[6] is about letting go of the illusion of control. It is a phase that invites us to get vulnerable, to expose our feelings, and open ourselves so that we can discover the fullest creative potential of our work.

WHEN THE WHEEL WON'T SPIN (Feeling Stuck)

We probably spent about 20 years stumbling around before we got to this place. Here are some fundamentals (from our personal learnings):

Embrace that the timing will always be right

This can move as fast or as slow as you'd like. You may have something specific that you're working on developing and want to take this wheel on a turn, or you may want to read this all in one go. It can click immediately or it needs to sit and wait and then in 6 months from now, there's an a-ha moment.

Be patient with yourself

If you find yourself feeling confused or annoyed by what comes up, sit with yourself and don't worry too much about what surfaces. It's not supposed to be stressful, and if it feels that way, take a break. The framework is about striving less; the work is actually being done as you read and reflect. Starting this is already taking that first step to harmonizing who you are.

---

[6] Macy, Joanna. "Entering the Bardo," *Emergence Magazine.*
https://emergencemagazine.org/op_ed/entering-the-bardo/. July 20, 2020.

Dismantle Mental Blocks

The practices that come up will ask you to speak your truth. If you are having a hard time doing so and see that there is a block, then try to write it down. Sit with a pen and spill things onto a page. You needn't read it again but allow yourself to meditate on the block and listen to what is needed for yourself. This is also useful for any triggers that may come up, too. See in Part III, the different exercises you can explore.

Understand Conflicts of Values

Triggers, emotions, the gut feeling that "something is not sitting right," can often come up in the everyday. The tension you feel and that partner you want to change, or that boss you're waiting to appreciate you, is really about being in a place where your values are not in alignment with the other person or the organization. You may have a strong justice value, and a conflict doesn't mean that justice doesn't matter at your

workplace, but it simply is something they may value less. The Wheel in many of its phases, asks you to turn to what you self-determine are your personal or team's core values.

Acknowledge Systemic Racism, Oppression, and the Patriarchy

It's hard to talk about self-care, imposter syndrome, gaslighting, and paying for therapy without acknowledging that women and other underrepresented groups are already suffering in a system that wasn't designed with their inclusion or success in mind. Love, light, and prayers won't alleviate the necessary rage and need for liberation from systems of oppression that are fighting to hang on.

Know How to Not Know

The point of the Wheel is getting you to a place where you begin to trust a deeper, quieter part of you. So if you don't know, that's OK! An admission of not-knowing is also a sign of great faith and trust. Uncertainty is the new normal. When you can identify that you don't know something, it means that when you need to know, you will know!

PHASE:
REFLECT

PHASE: REFLECT

The Incas are just one culture which believes that to live is to be integrated within the self. At its most basic, being self-integrated is about noticing and welcoming your wholeness. Integration as we refer to it here is a process of awakening into higher level perception and compassion. The acceptance of the light and the dark, the messy and the all-put-together. To express self-integration means showing up in your life, on the daily, as your whole self. All parts of you are welcome, all parts of you are invited, all parts of you are united and worthy of understanding and expression. You are being you in the most you way possible. You are a beacon of you-ness. You are a lighthouse that draws people and energy in toward the pillar of You. You have nothing to hide.

We don't just arrive at this understanding of our wholeness. This idea of self-integration implies there is a quest to get to this "integration." It is a journey and a process of reflection. To follow the path toward enlightenment and joy, we must unearth and stitch back together those aspects of ourselves that are hidden, unaddressed, buried, or otherwise obscured.

To REFLECT, we practice quieting the mind and stepping away from our habitual ways of being and thinking. We sit with ourselves. We sit without media or imminent distraction. Over time, reflective routines and rituals increase our resilience and make us conscious of the hidden beliefs and patterns that can hold us back. Reflection reveals our gifts and uncovers our vision.

ARCHETYPE: THE VISIONARY

While this has become an over-hyped, self-indulgent title, we're calling visionaries exactly what they are: people with the gift of seeing. It's a gift we all have, but we often don't have permission to use it. Visionary has been reserved for that certain Founder, the Captain of the Ship. And in a team or organization, it's assumed you can only have ONE. We've worked with a number of self-proclaimed visionaries. But if all you do is sit around and have visions, you might detach from reality. Are you going to do anything about the things you say you see? Do your visions have a positive or negative impact? And are they in service of the collective or of the ego?

In the in-between, visionaries get active. We want you to see this special gift IN YOU and use it creatively. There are so many ways to start on this important REFLECT phase, and we invite you to put on the Visionary hat and spend time beginning to feel and sense the things around you. Who are the people you are in a community and relationship with? How do you feel within your workplace? Even in this world? What do you hope for your future? What feels like it is on the horizon? You have your own dreams and need not wait for someone else to tell you what they should be for yourself.

THE PRACTICE

"Do not try to fix whatever comes in your life. Fix yourself in such a way that whatever comes, you will be fine." - Sadhguru

MINDFULNESS IS KEY

We are constantly messaged by people, brands, political interests, you name it. Every social media, or work platform algorithm is designed to mine our attention. As a leader and a teammate, it's incumbent on you to pause and analyze this aggressive intake if you want to cultivate discernment rather than just chasing the next shiny object, if you want to remain grounded rather than fall victim to targeted messaging.

Mindfulness builds awareness. Awareness allows us to slow down and notice. Regular practice is crucial. Meditation is one popular way of practicing mindfulness, but you don't need to sit on a cushion for 8 hours, fast for a week, or head to an ashram in order to practice. Maybe it looks more like mindful walking, coloring a coloring book, or piecing together a puzzle. It can be listening to lyric-free music, or going on a solo hike. What you are looking to create is space between you and your thoughts. In our frenetic world, our mind is the boss, and you become a servant to it. A state of mindfulness allows you to become aware of your thoughts and separate the voices of doubt, restlessness, general chatter, whatever. You meditate and rest in order to reconnect with who you really are -- to be out of the distraction of your mind's noise for a moment. To remind yourself that you are not your thoughts. There is a you behind, underneath, and around your thoughts. A you that is essential and present.

In start-up culture, the notion of the "chaotic" Founder or boss often gets excused because the organization is so crazed; the productivity creates so much demand. And that is true for just some. The remaining other CEOs and/or founders we've worked with, in truth, never knew how to take a moment to sit back and assess what was happening around them -- more importantly, the information that was arriving minute by minute. So engrossed in making sure their assistants packed their schedules, they never realized that decisions were being made simply based on the last conversation they had. Or that a whole business pivot, came from a trending Twitter article. Eventually the whole team would see this and their own trust in that leader dimmed as they questioned decision-making and direction not founded in reflection.

WHAT THIS PHASE EXPLORES

· **WHO AM I NOW?** Who are you really without the roles you play or the possessions you own? How do others describe you without nouns, job titles and identifiers?

· **WHAT DO I REALLY WANT?** The answers may be material, spiritual, ethereal, emotional, physical - anything you'd like to see fulfilled in your life.

· **WHAT IS MY PURPOSE? HOW CAN I USE MY GIFTS TO BE OF SERVICE?** What lights you up? Makes your heart dance? What are your innate gifts and how can you use them to bring happiness to yourself and others?

· **WHAT AM I GRATEFUL FOR?** What are the blessings in your life at this moment?

The process is not linear. It will never "feel" complete. There is no deadline or finish line. This is no rat race. You are not behind. There are infinite layers of knowing, and each time you engage in reflection, you peel back another layer. Each time you engage in reflection, that muscle of exploration and articulation gets stronger. This is great rep work. Your noticing of things about yourself begets more noticing and more noticing and more aha! Insights.

in-between

- Guru / Cult leadership

- Profit, stakeholders, ego

  - Work as identity; hard working ethic

  - Expert mindset

- Authoritarian/Hierarchy

  - Imposter syndrome, "fake it 'til you make it"

- Co-creator

- Co-op, shared, communal capitalism

- Servant, and authentic leadership

- Impact and in service of humanity and planet

- It takes a village, the community cultivates your gifts

- Vulnerable / servant leadership

desired state

AM I DONE?

The goal of this phase is to know yourself and check in with what you truly need. From there, you show up, express, and act on this authentic you. While reflection is infinite, and there are always more depths to plumb, you'll never quite feel "done," as more clarity comes with your development. Can you create a new rhythm in your life that offsets the chaos and noisiness of our collective reality? This practice is a balm. It may feel like just another commitment right now, but there does come a point where your reflective practice becomes so much a part of your daily situation that you miss it dearly when you skip a single day. Reflect is also the place where you can develop your "observer mind" to catch yourself being judgmental to you or your team. What is this underlying trigger? Is this situation about me or am I being projected upon? Is this emotion misplaced?

From a personal journey, this phase allowed a window to heal yourself, by seeing your wounds and allowing space for that healing.

The next phase of Design will ask you if you're ready to take your ideas to the next point of creation. Are you ready to take the idea and come up with the new invention? Have you found what you'd like to serve and are you ready to start building? Perhaps you will be in Design and realize, there's more to still reflect on, then your work can merge here, too.

PHASE:
DESIGN

PHASE: DESIGN

You're ready to create. You've reflected, gone inside, got quiet, and now's the time to get into the how after you've uncovered the why and what. There's a problem you are trying to solve, and many leaders and teams tend to skip the Reflect phase. They miss out on gaining an empathetic and thoughtful understanding of the problem when they are so quick to get to the "productivity" stage of things.

Understanding the problem, feeling grounded in the why, it's now time to build the invention or the solution! We've got assumptions, and now it's time to invent, create, experiment, and test it. Many would call this the ideation phase but we know we can't do this alone, so this is also about building our teams, our community and where we will seek help. Whether it's a new venture, or something personal, we will need to map out how we will get there.

What actually happens at this stage? What will we be doing as Inventors?

- Prototyping
- Canvassing and testing business and creative ideas
- Building a business plan
- Sketching the design, building, dress
- Drafting roadmaps, blueprints, pilot tests, table of contents, outlines
- Action steps for healing
- Finding a sense of meaning after trauma;
- Purpose through process
- Planning

The Tree of Life is a symbolic, ancient talisman that is represented in Buddhism, Judaism, Egyptian Kemeticism, and the Koran. The Kabala and Bodhi Tree are examples as trunks of strength, that connect our earth and spiritual realms. We honor the Tree of Life (and all trees) as natural reminders that nothing can grow, if not loved and nourished. We take care of the root systems and bring in solid preparation for any new growth and ideas that we want to see from start to finish.

ARCHETYPE: THE INVENTOR

Where the Visionary asked us to sit and imagine the new ways of work we want in the world, the INVENTOR frames and builds those visions into reality. Now that you have the kernel of your vision, what support or structures need to be mapped out to get to the finish line? In this phase, the invitation is to roll up our sleeves and get hands-on in the role of architecting the dream. Inventors have the energy and the ability to take risks with their work. Here's where we can enjoy experimenting, crafting, and creating!

This phase highlights the ways in which we must practice supporting and affirming ourselves. Trusting our inner wisdom can be a big change. Maybe we are used to expecting external validation or the approval of old structures or systems to tell us we are on the right path. The Inventor takes a proactive approach and considers every situation a gleeful experiment. There are no right or wrong paths, only discoveries. The Inventor leads with curiosity, aspiration and hope.

How will you interact with new ideas or unexpected circumstances and factor those into the design of your teams and solutions? In this new time, lean into self-trust and the spirit of digging in. It's a perfect time to connect to your inner strength to move your new ideas forward.

The Four Directions of the Medicine Wheel (Native American) and the Symbolism of the Directions.

The traditional, Native American Medicine Wheel circles around the individual, symbolic of the continuation of life. What goes around, comes around. This Wheel is represented by four cardinal directions and represents strengths and weaknesses, and what you need to learn and gain.

East direction: Spring or new beginnings, it's where the Sun rises and represents the dawn and arrival and is associated with the element of air. This is at a time of creativity and spirituality. With the dawn, it represents your inner visionary. Clarity, new ideas, visualizations.

South direction: Summer, adolescence. Abundance! It's experimentation and a time to build. The element here is fire, and hard work is paying off. For aboriginal peoples, the South also represents healing.

West direction: Autumn, our adult years; value setting and our own decisions. The element here is water, and for indigenous Europeans, this direction represented personal power and transformational change. It is the fall, and a time to regroup and purge.

North: Winter, rest, enlightenment, we become elders, and time to return/connect with the spirit world. The element here is earth, and we honor the winter. It's an hibernation and self-reflection period.

THE PRACTICE

The work of this phase is to align your vision to a set of action steps. First, take a moment to connect deeply with this dream of yours. Maybe the dream is yours alone or perhaps you share it with a team or an entire organization. What feelings does this vision evoke in you? How does your special perspective give juice to this vision? What draws you to this vision over and over?

How you enter this planning phase, and how you feel as you are designing, is as important as the outcome. How you feel influences what solutions you identify, which opportunities you see. Our moods define our perspective. A 2013 study sponsored by the National Institutes of Health reported, "Emotion determines how we perceive our world, organize our memory, and make important decisions."[7] The How of the planning process is as critical as What we are planning. The invitation is to stay nimble and relaxed, giving our teams and peers space to do the same. In this way, our perspective stays wide, engaged, open to a variety of possibilities.

The inventor brings ideas to fruition with playfulness. This person creates the first map, the first plan or strategy. The spirit of the process will carry the team and project forward. Whatever method you choose, remember that design and ideation is an iterative journey. There may be many cycles of refinement along the way. Prioritize flexibility, collegiality, and co-creation. If your team can flail and have fun in the midst of design, this translates to engagement and impact for your dream.

[7] Brosch, Tobias & Scherer, Klaus & Grandjean, Didier & Sander, David. (2013). *The impact of emotion on perception, attention, memory, and decision-making.* Swiss Medical Weekly. 143, 10.4414/smw.2013.13786

in-between

- 5-10 year plan

- Single visionary

- Economics over people

- Expectation of predictability

- Fear-based leadership

- Ends justify the means

- Expert mindset

- Are we done yet?!

- 1-2 year plans with 6 month contingencies

- Co-creation

- Team profit-sharing; collective abundance

- Being adaptive and agile

- Distributed responsibility

- Aligning with purpose

- Process = outcome

- Shift from "what can I own" to "what can we create together"

- Next level, growth mindset thinking

- Fluidity in identity, race, abilities and community.

- Enjoy the process

desired state

95.

The powerful, ancient, Eightfold Path of Buddhism is the predecessor to modern day team charter, core values, and integrity statements.

THE EIGHTFOLD PATH OF BUDDHISM:

1. Right understanding and viewpoint (based on the Four Noble Truths).
2. Right values and attitude (compassion rather than selfishness).
3. Right speech (don't tell lies, avoid harsh, abusive speech, avoid gossip).
4. Right action (help others, live honestly, don't harm living things, take care of the environment).
5. Right work (do something useful, avoid jobs which harm others).
6. Right effort (encourage good, helpful thoughts, discourage unwholesome, destructive thoughts).
7. Right mindfulness (be aware of what you feel, think and do).
8. Right concentration (practice meditation, unification of the mind.

WHAT THIS PHASE EXPLORES

- What do I yearn to create or transform?
- Where can I experiment?
- Why would someone want this problem solved?
- What can I uniquely contribute? Where do I see gaps that require help?
- What is the culture of the team I'd like to work with?
- What can be accomplished now?
- Who do I need to forge relationships with?
- Do these plans solve the problem?
- What is my motivation? What is my team's motivation?

AM I DONE?

We've seen it happen both ways: a team is so excited to get things done that they move too quickly to the next phase and immediately want to move to action, to the Enact phase, when the idea is still just half-baked and the group hasn't come together to see the full picture. It happens with poor change management or sudden pivots by insecure leadership. On the other end of the spectrum, a team can spend so much time in design and endless iteration that time is wasted as they seek the elegant, perfect solution when they need to ship.

You will know you are done
with Design when you
can articulate the drivers
that motivate you and/or
the team. When there is a
structure emerging for the
project, and the purpose is
clear. Perhaps the business
plan is vetted and ready
to send out. The roughest
outline for the novel is
jotted down. A clue that
the team has reached the
end of the design phase is
sometimes the repetition
of ideas - sometimes new
ideas slow to a drip and you
notice the team begin to
go round and round. Once
the design hasn't changed
fundamentally through a
couple of iterations, that is
a signal that this phase is
complete (for now).

TECH ADDICTION/ STAYING FOCUSED
Today's obsession with tech can hurt our
progress. Besides intellectual downgrade
(memory issues, inability to discern others'
emotions), what really affects us is our ability to
focus. We've become a distracted humanity.

Here's a few tips for setting proper boundaries:

1. Keep your bedroom a screen-free zone. An
old-school clock is a great way to wake up.
2. Don't run to your phone, Slack or emails as
soon as you wake up. Make that cup of coffee,
hop in the shower, try meditating. Set some
distance upfront or your inbox will determine
your day.
3. Delete apps. Periodically audit and remove.
Consider moving social media off your phone
and check it (if you must) over your laptop.
4. Turn off notifications and/or set time
boundaries.
5. Quit it cold-turkey! Think of those other
things you love to do and re-prioritize.

PHASE:
ENACT

"Leadership is about individuals. In fact, leadership is a distributed or collective capacity in a system, not just something that individuals do. Leadership is about the capacity of the whole system to sense and actualize the future that wants to emerge."
- Otto Scharmer, Leading from the Emerging Future: From Ego-System to Eco-System Economies

PHASE: ENACT

During Reflect we identified what we truly desired and intended. We then moved into Design where we articulated and iterated the requirements, constraints, and details of what we wanted to build. The Enact phase is about our readiness to take that design plan out into the real world, into tangible activity, into experiment and context. You may have already brainstormed with others, thought about who a co-founder could be, or uncovered a storm of books you want to explore. Here in Enact, we galvanize and bring the pieces together. Whether we are seeking to gather audiences, partners we hope to design alliances of work and joy with, or the internal parts of ourselves that are ready to shift... This is the moment we turn from Inventor to Conductor, to make the shi(f)t happen.

Enact may be an easy place for many to jump to because our culture is built on doing and making -- ACTION yields rewards. The doing-ness of our lives is prioritized in the work world and on social media, with systems of tasks to complete and achievements to unlock, family outings to showcase, and DIYs to document. Enact implies control and direction, check lists, Asana and Trello boards. But the true vibe of Enact is much broader.

In taking on the archetype of the Conductor, we are orchestrators. We are ready to execute and launch the agreed-upon design. Instead of being performative, "fake-busy," the work is thoughtful, collaborative. This is often a phase where fear can creep in: the self-doubt, the long checklist of details that may start to feel daunting; the spinning plates, the questioning of whether all the stars will align... This phase requires patience, commitment, and perseverance. It isn't just one long to-do list. It's a symphony, and you are moving with the music.

Enact need not be the scary part of what we build, solve, or create. In some ways, it is less important than the preparation that brought us to this moment. We are nearing the top of the roller coaster and about to come down. Perhaps it's not fear we feel, but the excitement of, holy shit, we are doing this! Enact can feel nerve-wracking -- Will this work? Is this the right team? Can I shake off what I've been conditioned to do so that I might jump into the unknown? And yet, there is so much joy in executing on something we believe in. All it takes is small steps forward in the direction of your desire.

103.

ARCHETYPE: THE CONDUCTOR

The Conductor receives the baton from the Inventor. The Conductor is often seen as just the executor, or the doer. However, the Conductor plays a crucial role in ensuring that we have moved from a passive place as a reactor, to one of initiation and growth. It is the chance for you to really power up: seed your life in the image of what you want to be doing and building. It's the powerful moment to integrate all your quirks, idiosyncrasies, and the sensitive spots that make up YOU. What is so special is that you are now embodying this maverick spirit, a unique blend of your wisdom and gifts. The Conductor archetype reminds us to

104.

move from intention to focus and execution.

This archetype allows us to take command of the spinning plates and notice how each task is intertwined and interdependent. The Conductor sees the view of the entire ecosystem and knows the whole system is greater than the sum of its parts. The Conductor leads with focus, determination and practicality.

How will you maintain your attention to what matters? Understanding the relationships between all the moving parts, and motivating those parts to create in harmony is the strength of the Conductor.

THE PRACTICE

We've arrived at the doing -- the let's get shit done -- phase. For the majority of us, this is what we know and where we feel most in control. We have certain skill sets that we are hired to do and this is essentially us just putting those skills to use and doing our jobs. This phase is about the dreams coming to fruition and the work finally manifesting. You're pulling together the resources: money, team, systems, etc. You've activated a group of professionals to help you get some past baggage sorted. Your work schedule has been rearranged, and you know how to prioritize those creative projects above all else. But in all that doing, the Wheel asks you to place intention in every step of the process as you build and create this new chapter; it's intentional work.

In terms of the "what," this will vary based on what you're building but the goal is to be intentional, consistent and determined about completion. And most importantly: take the risks you need to, in service of the dream.

This can be any of the following:

- Completing a roadmap or plan
- Hiring a team
- Finishing your art studio so you finally have space to start your work
- Signing up for that dating app
- Attending your first AA meeting
- Hiring a coach
- Signing the office lease
- Getting married (or breaking up)
- Running your first mile (or incorporating mid-day naps into your day)
- Quitting your job and sending that resume

What does mindful productivity entail?
Buddhism reminds us of the path to least resistance. To choose what flows and what feels joyful. Essentially, get back to basics! Here are some tips to ease you in during this practice.

- Mission Critical Tasks - Focus on one thing at a time

- Choose the easy things to start with
- Identify what needs to get done
- Prioritize and give yourself / your team deadlines
- Be accountable
- Be in flow and build categories of work e.g. Admins (emails, calls, etc.) in the morning and strategy (brainstorm, reading, reflection) midday.

WHAT THIS PHASE EXPLORES

- What is my motivation and intention to act?
- What do I want to launch?
- Who do I need to call? Who will help me? Who do I need to show up for me?
- Am I acting from a place of calm? Fear? Urgency?
- If urgent, how real is that urgentness?
- Do you feel at ease when you think about the project?
- Does it scare you just the right amount? (Remember you are trying something new here, so it should feel like a bit of a stretch, a little uncomfortable; that is how you know you are pursuing a growth area.)
- How might I expand my circle of influence?
- What do I want to amplify?
- What do I already have at the ready?

in-between

- Collapsing structures based on institutional racism

- Relying on existing resources and support systems

- Founder-centric

- Same old job descriptions and employee "type"

- "This is what I did at my old company"

- Work-life balance is a false binary

- Separatism

- Systems of community, growth, on behalf of improving the collective

- Alternative resource and supplies; e.g. different ideas for capitalism

- Collaborative; co-op model; profit sharing

- Unity consciousness

- Hire for growth mindset; diversity backgrounds in work experience as well

- "Here's the new challenge I want to explore as a team"

- Integrated, connected teams honoring the personal and professional

desired state

AM I DONE?

We are working with a nonlinear framework, a cycle. So in one sense, you will never be done experimenting. But in another sense, your particular phase of ENACT (for example, in the co-creation of a team charter) can be completed as a single iteration. Regardless, you may feel fear. You may feel a bit uncomfortable or uneasy because you are launching a Thing. And if you've done the work in the reflection and design phases, chances are that the launch you are contemplating is for something that feels like a little more of a stretch.

Maybe you are ready to enact something that challenges the notions of how your team works traditionally. Maybe your idea is disruptive to the dominant management style or the culture of the industry you professionally grew up inside. Do the best you can to launch your minimum viable experiment into the world with the same passion that drew you to it in the first place.

PHASE:
ALLOW

"Before I was clever and I wanted to change the world. Today I am wise, so I am changing myself." -Rumi

PHASE: ALLOW

Allowing, like letting go, sometimes connotes surrender, weakness, or complacency. To allow is in tension with our western values of autonomy, independence, and ambition. Typically we are rewarded for that doing energy, for productivity. In the extreme, we have become such collateral damage of capitalism that we've replaced real joy with our list of KPIs. So what then is the value of allowing?

Allow is a pause. It is the phase where you must let go and trust. Allow is about setting our creations free in the world. It is where we give ourselves, our teams, and our projects the space they need to develop.

Allowing is practicing trust. Trust that things are in motion just as you've worked hard for them to be. Trust in yourself that your aim is true. By relinquishing control we say, "We have faith in what we have imagined."

Allow is an intentional state of be-ing, (as opposed to do-ing). It is a "deliberate and elegant practice," as a meditation teacher put it. It is the moment after we have completed something when we get to take a breath.

- By allowing, we are trusting our instincts and following our gut
- We are open to possibilities and prepared for surprises
- To pause and make space for the change to happen
- You've done the work now, let the Universe take over
- Releasing the old story
- To prepare yourself for a new engagement
- To receive
- Relax into the unfolding; some religions refer to this as "faith"

THE ARCHETYPE: STEWARD

The Steward archetype has its roots as a caretaker of the land, a nice groundskeeper in retirement. But the Steward we invite here is an active and empathetic champion of the cause or community. She is a leader here to hold space for the whole of the planet, people and spirit. The Steward embodies the collective and protects the system.

The Steward is a self-aware leader; an individual who commits to self-actualization. They shepherd the groups' mission but also see how society is greater than the self.

In this role as Steward, you are allowing your team to make the mistakes it is ready to make. You are modeling for them what it means to be on the path. Growth rather than perfection or control. You provide guidance, support, but mostly, allow and let go.

THE PRACTICE

How might we begin "allowing?" Here is some guidance we use:

1. Be gentle with yourself. The change you are already undergoing is real. Give yourself the benefit of the doubt that you are doing the best you can.

2. Trust your intuition. The timing is right, the inner guidance is true. Meditation allows you to hear it.

3. Open yourself to receiving: messages, answers, feedback, the fruits of your labor.

4. Practice flexibility. Let go of self-judgment and expectations when you notice them.

5. Find or create daily rituals that give you comfort or create space for the team.

6. Experiment with creative embodiment to keep energy moving: walk it out, dance, etc.

7. Are you ready and willing to be satisfied? What does success look like?

Taoism teaches that the living you are now doing can fully express your nature. It's the core of the human experience: to live and simply BE. In your discovery of Taoist practices, one learns that we own nothing, and that we are just a passing custodian of items outside of our nature. We are stewards and we are vessels. The acceptance of your life; follow your breath to find peace. Release expectations.

WHAT THIS PHASE EXPLORES

There's a leadership mantra we love about ALLOW: "Hold on tightly, let go lightly." How does one hold on to their dream and still let go and allow things to unfold? For most of us, letting go is the most difficult, sometimes most terrifying, thing. In the workplace, our "normal" is often project managing or micro-managing every detail from every perspective so that we feel a sense of order, a semblance of control over the outcome. Think of that inventor that has created something and they're unable to let go of the worry and the negative fantasies of everything that could go wrong. A big part of ALLOW is about letting circumstances have time and space to unfold. Not rushing the process. This doesn't mean stopping or quitting when things feel tight. Allowing is focusing on the trust as the work may ebb and flow, and to stop ourselves

from spiraling when we get triggered.

Another aspect of ALLOW is the letting go of all ideas, relationships, What's the Difference Between Allow and Reflect?

As we progress around the Wheel and move out of the phase of Allow, we arrive back at the phase of Reflection. Both of these phases might seem abstract or a bit nebulous. The energy of them both is contemplative and has more to do with our state of being than any given activity or specific practice.

While encouraging deeper awareness, and spending more time in states of conscious awareness (read: not on autopilot or crazy multi-tasking), the work in Allow is to learn to let go and trust, and in Reflect, we are learning to sit quietly in order to visualize the new.

Ways these phases are different:

ALLOW
Surrender and trust
Detaching from the agenda
Give up the illusion that we are in control
Receiving

REFLECT
Identify core values for us and our team
Setting our internal agenda
Identify the illusions keeping us caged
Finding authenticity and purpose

AM I DONE?

ALLOW also means it is OK to relax. How can that even be possible? Let go of the pictures of your ideal self or team in an ideal world. You've done the work; the reflection, design and enacting. Let go of the story. Re-enter the flow of life with a new sense of groundedness. By allowing, you usher in the real transformation. If you can't let go, you won't be able to tune into the feedback, messages and receive rewards when you spiral with worry. It is in these moments between projects, after major events, even in the pause between meetings, where you can see where some space appears, allowing the continuity to be interrupted, and to end any false projection that was placed on ourselves and the work.

The new measuring stick for how we move forward is "How does it feel?" This question points to the practice of pausing and noticing your feelings in any given situation or when faced with a decision. How your emotions and thoughts show up in your body, for example, are powerful data to guide your actions. Do you notice you are allowing your feelings to surface and move through you? Are you choosing positivity or negativity? If you answered "yeah," then chances are you are getting better at allowing. It's working. Lead with the heart and not with the hustle.

AS THE WHEEL TURNS

This circular framework is a way to support your personal awakening and new team work habits. The exercises and questions on the Wheel place great importance on candor, openness, agility, and co-creative relationships. One practical upside to working the Wheel is that investments you make in one phase will spill over into another. For example, your reflective practice will improve how you articulate what is important to you, which can ease and smooth team communications when it comes to designing the end product.

You might choose to revisit the Wheel on a certain time interval (e.g., monthly, quarterly) to examine how your plans and priorities have shifted over time. A common agile team exercise is to conduct a "retrospective" after the completion of a milestone. This gives everyone a chance to check in with themselves and their expectations. Perhaps the collective vision has a new focal point, different constraints or a shifting context. Take stock of where you or the team need the most support, and make a commitment to revisit these exercises regularly. Put it on the calendar!

You are not alone here. We are in the thicket between these old and new ways. But we can forge new thought habits together. We can create habitats of nourishment and purpose. As agents of change, we are the architects of our experience and our context. Staying off autopilot, maintaining self-awareness, and pausing to notice old stories that don't serve us or the vision.

Who says humanity can't learn as fast as the changes we've already set in motion? Let's invite our learning and reflection to grow exponentially. Let's scale thoughtfulness, care and wholeness. Let's weave compassion for self and others into each activity we do at work. May each phase of the Wheel deepen our understanding of ourselves and the whole.

III. PLAY & PRACTICE

"...that we are each other's harvest: we are each other's business: we are each other's magnitude and bond." - Gwendolyn Brooks, "Paul Robeson," The Collected Works of Gwendolyn Brooks

Take a moment to notice where the Wheel or the practices have sparked more curiosity in you. What piques your interest? Have you identified a new need for yourself or your organization? This section of exercises is a spot to explore a bit more.

We start off with a slew of practices that we relied on as managers to help us establish effective, high-trust teams. Next, we introduce the seemingly woo-woo but actually quite practical concepts of abundance and ritual -- and how you might utilize them at work. Finally, we leave you with some thoughts on leadership, no matter where you are in the organization.

In the In-Between, we invite you to think way outside the box. Many of the processes we've used in the past to motivate or engage people, manage projects, or do the job just don't work in this new reality. It may feel uncomfortable at first to try something new; this is how you know it's a learning edge. If you need support, find a trusted colleague who shares your enthusiasm to experiment with these types of participatory and reflective activities.

HOW WE SHOW UP

Now the fun stuff: the actual PRACTICE (and the work)! Think of the offerings here as small experiments toward shifting the ways we work and think. As we mentioned earlier, there is both a doing energy and a being energy. We hope through these exercises to honor and hold space for both sides of the coin. In each section we share our favorite resources, affirmations and juicy questions as we journey around the Wheel.

We call this section "Play" because there is joy and liberation in the act of discovery. Play creates a dynamic of curiosity and openness. Exercises, experiments, and resources are organized by each of the four phases of the Wheel: Reflect, Design, Enact, and Allow. The practices can be done individually or as a small group. We're sharing these "classics" as they've yielded amazing results time and time again. Consider these a baseline, the beginnings of your path to a new way of working.

In each section of Play, you'll find in the following that corresponds to each Phase:

- Favorite Resources
- Reflection Questions
- Affirmations
- Visualization Exercises
- Treasured Practices

Different experiences will arise from these exercises. Know that the work we are doing on an individual or team level is all part of the important progress happening on a planetary scale.

Reminders as you make your way:

- Ground yourself. Take care of your mental and physical space
- Be conscious and mindful. Lead with your heart, release the "productivity" mind-set
- Be good to yourself. If you catch yourself in judgment, be gentle
- Trust yourself. If you ask if you're doing it right, the answer is no. Because there is no wrong way of doing this
- You are enough but be prepared to change
- Seek out a green space - even a small corner park or a potted plant
- Drink water

VISUALI-ZATION

One tool we make great use of is visualization. Visualization is a powerful way of reflecting and exercising your imagination. To jumpstart the magic of future-casting, we like to use visualization. We offer a specific visualization exercise in each phase of the Wheel as a means of pointing us toward the future with sensory details. When we envision, we are building the muscle of creativity. Neuroscience tells us that envisioning has a different chemical signature in our brains than mere problem-solving. While problem-solving is often stress or fear-based, the act of envisioning releases more joyful or love-based neurochemical through the brain's Reticular Activating System (RAS)[8], a matrix that creates an important filter for what makes you happy.

Using images, archetypes, stories, and symbols helps to open up this sliver of access to our greater magical thoughts:
- They are signposts and tools we use to journey into this realm of the not-yet, of the just being born, of that which is being reenvisioned

- Stories and symbols are the language of imagination, how imagination is expressed

- Imagination is also a gateway to the stories which live in the field (collective unconscious)

- Imagination is one of the first steps of manifestation -- science fiction brought us the satellite, the internet, and many other things far before they were invented and brought into the "real" world

[8] Midbrain. B.L Walter and A.G. Shaikh. *Encyclopedia of the Neurological Science* (Second Edition), pp. 28-33. 2014.

PHASE 1:
REFLECT

PHASE I: REFLECT

INWARD > OUTWARD

In this new world, we choose to lead by our hearts rather than being led by our brains, thought habits, or the proverbial "hustle." That means reconnecting inward to what is most important to us and who we truly are. Our work can be driven by purpose and intention as opposed to the need to stay busy or so-called productive. The Reflect phase is an opportunity to get clear on the underlying purpose and motivation for a project, relationship, team, or new idea.

GOING DEEP

Our energy is limited. The deeper and more honestly you are able to reflect on your motivations, understanding personal and your team's boundaries, the better equipped you will be in determining how to move forward and where you want to expend energy. If you've got only so many quivers for your bow, get clear about your target. Reflecting on your mark will only make your efforts more efficient.

FAVORITE RESOURCES

These books and workshops span a wide range of traditions and approaches to reflection. Move toward what piques your curiosity. These are some broad resources, but certainly seek out the many great teachers that also speak to specific audiences (gender specific, LGBTQIA+, POC, etc.)

- *Society for Shamanic Practices* (workshops, training)
- *A New Earth*, *The Power of Now*, Eckhart Tolle
- *Seat of the Soul*, Gary Zukav
- *Change Your Thoughts, Change Your Life: Living the Wisdom of the Tao*, Wayne Dyer
- *Buddhism Plain and Simple*, Steve Hagan

- *Tibetan Book of the Dead*, various
- *Managing Yourself*, Harvard Business Review
- *Daring Greatly*, Brené Brown
- *Ask and It Is Given*, Esther and Jerry Hicks
- *Wishes Fulfilled: Mastering the Art of Manifesting*, Wayne Dyer
- *The Science of Getting Rich, The Science of Being Great*, Books by Wallace D. Wattles
- *E-Squared: Nine Do-It-Yourself Energy Experiments That Prove Your Thoughts Create Your Reality*, Pam Grout

REFLECTION QUESTIONS

We give you lots of questions to noodle on in this particular phase. If you aren't sure where to begin your reflection, try journaling or recording a voice memo on your phone or computer. Answer 2-3 of the questions below if any call to you, or write questions of your own.

- What do I love most right now?
- What am I longing for in life?
- What's one change I could make to give me peace?
- What do I need to give myself permission to do?
- How am I taking care of myself?
- What does life look like when everything works in harmony?
- Where do I feel resistance?
- What sensations do I experience in my body when I am sitting still?
- What do I feel called to do?
- Where can I feel my breath moving in my body?
- What can I let go of?
- What would I love to never do again?
- What's weighing me down?
- I'm fantasizing about radically changing

---------- .

- What's dead in the water? What has lost traction?
- Who or what am I tolerating, putting up with, or settling for?

AFFIRMATIONS

Reciting affirmations out loud in front of a mirror can change your thought patterns and develop a more resilient brain that better adapts to challenges.[9] There are affirmations accompanying each phase of the framework. They pull our focus back toward the present moment.

- I breathe my breath. My breath breathes me.
- I am connected to everything.
- As within, so without, as above, so below.
- I am at peace with myself.
- I recognize I am the only one who can do the work I've been called to do.
- Be here now.
- Peace is available to me at all times.
- I give myself permission to follow my purpose.
- I am worthy of reflection.
- I give myself permission to shine.
- I am ready to receive.

BUDDHISM'S 3 UNIVERSAL TRUTHS

Everything in life is impermanent and always changing.

Because nothing is permanent, a life based on possessing things or persons doesn't make you happy.

There is no eternal, unchanging soul and "self" is just a collection of changing characteristics or attributes.

[9] Cascio, Christopher N., Matthew Brook O'Donnell, Francis J. Tinney, Matthew D. Lieberman, Shelley E. Taylor, Victor J. Strecher, and Emily B. Falk. "Self-affirmation activates brain systems associated with self-related processing and reward and is reinforced by future orientation," *Social Cognitive and Affective Neuroscience.* pp. 621-629; doi: 10.1093/scan/nsv136. 2016.

VISUALIZATION EXERCISE

As with all these visualizations, we recommend recording them by reading into your phone or laptop - or corral one of your sweet-voiced friends, colleagues or loved ones to read them into your voice memos for playback later.

Find a comfortable and straight-backed position, either sitting upright in a chair or laying down on a mat or bed. From this space, we will be moving into a practice of grounding and then quiet reflection. Begin by taking 3 deep breaths in through the nose and out through the mouth. Try to clear any old air in your lungs. Take a moment to notice or feel the circulation of the new air in your chest. Out with the old air, in with the new.

Now close your eyes if that feels relaxing. Bring your thoughts to the bottoms of your feet. Are they flat on the floor? Where do your feet touch

a surface? Quietly, and without judgment, simply notice the places and spaces your feet or your body are touching the ground or another surface. Allow yourself to sink into these spaces and let the ground or the bed or the chair support you. On the next exhale, drop your shoulders. Notice any places in your body that may still be holding some tension, and gently ask those parts to release.

As you relax into your posture and into your body, I invite you to imagine yourself at the edge of a tranquil shallow pool.

Take a moment to imagine the setting - perhaps it is wooded, or maybe it is a tropical locale, whatever you like. The water looks warm and inviting and you have this beautiful sanctuary all to yourself. The air is pleasant and you sink your bare toes into the water. It's the perfect temperature - whatever you like best. It's so relaxing just to wiggle your toes in the water.

As your feet relax in the water, imagine the warmth as it travels up your legs and throughout your whole body, up through all of your limbs, and up along your spine, into your neck and jaw and head. Let the warmth further relax and restore you.

This water refuels and restores and ignites. It holds any weight you may carry and gives you nutrients. From this place of stillness and quiet, take another deep breath in and out. Perhaps you can imagine this beautiful blue water infusing each part of you, filling you up with positive energy. If you find your mind wandering, just turn your attention back

to your breath, or the image of the warm water moving against your body.

- What are you noticing now?
- What are you feeling curious about?
- What sensations do you notice in your body? What message might they have?
- What do you have gratitude for at this moment?

As you reflect on these questions, give yourself a few minutes to daydream about each one. Take a few more deep breaths. When you are ready to finish this practice, gently wiggle your fingers and toes to come back into your space. Now slowly open your eyes.

DAILY REFLECTION PRACTICES

Selecting and committing to a daily contemplative practice helps you to slow down and regain quiet in service to a bigger, more fulfilled you.

Goal: Every day, 5 minutes. You can do this!

Set Intention. An important first step is setting an intention for a personal or group reflection. An intention is a conscious message we tell ourselves to direct and focus our exploration. Here are some sample intentions around reflection:
Learning to speak up for myself
Learning to listen and be more considerate
Noticing my limiting beliefs
Identifying and working through triggers with my team
Being truthful v. being nice or a people-pleaser

If you are struggling to come up with an intention for your reflection, ask yourself any of these questions:

- What has been on your mind?
- What do you feel drawn to?
- Where do you feel energy and curiosity?
- Where would you like to have a discovery?
- What aspects of yourself feel murky or itchy?
- Where is your learning edge?
- What is becoming clear?

Set Your Attention. We first asked you to set an intention so that you'd feel comfy, like, OK I can do this action item, this feels normal, this feels usual.

This next step is not about doing but BEING. It is about setting our attention. It is about noticing and improving the quality of our attention. This involves slowing down. Slowing down is about bringing breath and space and even boredom into the mix. It is getting quiet enough to hear the smaller voices and insights. It is about setting down your phone and unplugging altogether, even if we are talking two minutes to start. Put your phone in another room. Go now. We'll wait here...

Investigate what came up.
You have prepared yourself to reflect by setting an intention. You have slowed down your pace and become aware of the quality of your attention. You got quiet. You sat with it. Go you! Now is the step where you ask... what came up? What emerged, even if you only sat still for 5 minutes? What surprised you? What felt good and what felt icky? (the contrasts are important!) Record or write down any insights or a-ha! moments, or talk it out with a colleague or friend.

NOTE: If you are setting up a daily practice for your whole team
Make sure it is part of your alliance or team charter -- that everyone buys in, feels safe.
Share the purpose of the reflection -- to give folx a break, or to help the team focus? Ask the team for suggestions on what things could use a little more reflective energy.
Keep the time. Be considerate of adding another task for people. If it's 5 minutes, make it so. Sense into it, be in experimentation mode. Try it for a couple weeks and if it doesn't take for the whole group, don't force it. You might make it optional from the beginning, and see how the practice evolves.

TREASURED PRACTICES

This snapshot annotated list represents some of our treasured reflective practices. These are all time-tested and have played a big part in our own evolution and how we've worked with teams and clients over the years. That said, it is not exhaustive by any means, and we invite further exploration of diverse traditions and resources for methods of reflection, self-analysis, and healing.

"Meditation means dissolving the invisible walls that unawareness has built." -Sadhguru

MEDITATION (SITTING)

Meditation can be fucking hard. Who has time for even 10 minutes of each day? Your mind wanders to the to-do list, or it's hard to get calm. But meditation isn't about "no thoughts, no mind." It's about stillness to separate the many voices, lists, to-dos, fears that come through. You are meditating to reach nirvana, you're meditating to LET GO. Which of your thoughts belong to the authentic you, which belongs to the critical, egoic you? Or your parents' expectations? Or societal norms? To sit, we let go of any of our past anchors, thoughts, feelings, and stories in order to digest lessons learned. The power of meditation, sitting and quietly listening, is the fuel for your future. Reflection is hard. It's letting go, parsing through shadow work and fighting the old wounds that come through as fear. We find that if we're able to sit for even 15 minutes at the start of the day, that calmness can take us through obstacles and stress that can come up later throughout the day. Any type of daily sitting practice allows us to get closer to our intuition and begin hearing the voice of our own inner guidance more clearly. We are not meditating to get to far-off enlightenment, we are meditating to get back to a place of awareness. Learning to slow down and trust the knowledge and wisdom inside us can break through old habits or untruths that are not serving us. There are so many different forms of meditation. (We have the most experience with secular Buddhism). Eyes open or closed. Incense or not. Guidance or none. The core idea is to sit in quiet, and release. Focus on the breath. When chattering thoughts and interruptions and sensations arise, THAT'S OK. Just notice it and then pull your focus back to the breath. Here are three basic steps:

1) Take a seat (keep a straight back or lie down)
2) Place your attention on your breath
3) When you notice the mind wander, label 'thinking,' and return to your breath

Your thoughts will wander far and wide. If you feel frustrated, forgive yourself over and over. We have to remember not to judge ourselves for the 50,000 times our mind strays in 5 minutes. Yes, that is the practice. That is the whole point. Not to be perfect at it, but to show up. Let's revel in our imperfectness and smile at ourselves each time we notice our minds straying. Keep at it.

MORNING PAGES (FREE WRITING)

Borrowed from the inimitable Julia Cameron and *The Artist's Way*, morning pages are a reflective practice that involves longhand writing three pages first thing in the morning, stream of consciousness. Think of it as a writing meditation. The writing itself may be of no importance -- you can burn it, keep it, or continue to evolve it. The point of the exercise is to make a habit of filling three longhand pages (takes 20-30 minutes) to dump out whatever is in your brain. Don't worry about grammar, logic, or style. This is just about writing out the words that flow immediately to your mind, stream of consciousness.

MOVEMENT (DANCING, SINGING, CHANTING)

A more embodied and less thinky means of reflection is simply instituting a practice of 5 minutes of all-out dancing (think of a muppet waving their limbs around maniacally, and you get the idea), or singing your face off. Go to a room where you can be alone (or sing inside your car or the shower). Blast the music if you feel like shaking it, or pick a sad song and bawl your eyes out. When the song is over, you will find that there is a lovely empty space leftover. In that space, things will emerge.

CHANTING OM

1. Take an upright seated or standing position.

2. Turn your left palm up and keep it close to your navel...

3. Close your eyes and invite relaxation...

4. After a deep inhale, exhale and make the sound "OM."

5. Feel the vibrations of your breath and voice that run through the body.

6. Once you have paid attention to the sounds and vibrations in your body, breathe in and count to five.[10]

BREATHWORK

Another practice of mindfulness and adjacent to meditation, breathwork is a practice of conscious, controlled breathing done especially for relaxation, meditation, or therapeutic purposes (Merriam-Webster). Some breathwork practices create states of clarity, intense aliveness and even ecstasy. Sometimes breathwork is done in conjunction with other practices. Prānāyāma, for example, is the practice of breath control in yogic traditions. Practicing with your Prana, or breath, can be as simple as slowing down to intentionally notice the space between your inhale and your exhale. In order to become aware of this in-between moment - one must find a moment of stillness.

---

[10] Sandhu, Devakar. "What is the correct way to chant OM?," *Yogapedia*.
https://www.yogapedia.com/what-is-the-correct-way-to-chant-om/7/10878.

POISON PEN LETTERS

This practice is about releasing that which we are enraged about. One of our coaching teachers said these letters are about "what you can't be with!" These are letters you write to the people or situations that burn you up, make you crazy, put you in tears. Write a letter and say all of the mean and crazy things you've ever wanted to say to or about the thing or person. Give yourself the permission to go all out. Pour it out. The pages may be tear-streaked and dog-eared. Keep going, get it all out. When you are finished, you can burn or shred, toss or otherwise destroy the letter as a sign you are releasing these feelings. This release is a means of reflection, allowing us to exorcize the bad thoughts and feelings we experience, yet rarely allow ourselves to acknowledge and process. Note: We don't recommend ever sending these letters.

ABUNDANCE

We are all Creators. Everything that exists in the world, every product, service, or concept was once just the seed of an idea in someone's mind. It's all made up. Even money is a human invention! And yet, many of us still feel a limitation in regard to what's possible. We put conditions on our own growth and success, many times without realizing it. Whether that stems from childhood or institutional structures that created these rules, we were taught to accept we had and not dream any further.

But the universe does want to give us what we desire. Can we invest a little time and energy into stretching our dreams a bit, our definitions of what is possible? How might you shift your thinking from a place of yearning and lack to a sense of presence and gratitude for what we see all around us? Establishing and tending your relationship to abundance is key to inviting flow and opportunity.

When you are feeling abundant and grateful already, you are more likely to be in a growth mindset, more likely to identify opportunities and promises you see in your immediate environment. The exercises below help to get you or the team into a more appreciative frame of reference, which can be very helpful when strategizing for the future, or building culture.

ABUNDANCE EXERCISES

Vision Board. What wild and delicious things do you want to invite into your personal abundance? Make a physical or virtual collage, or pinboard of the images, words, ideas, people, and positive feelings that exemplify your personal definition of abundance. Include only the images, ideas, or words that make you buzz or zing - the things that spark joy and feel like a whole body Yes. Hang it somewhere you can see it daily.

Daydream Spendsheet.

This exercise is incredibly powerful for loosening the reins of your imagination and revealing some of your deepest yearnings. This exercise requires a commitment every day for two weeks. It only takes a couple minutes a day, but requires a little preparation. The idea here is to get dreams flowing around what you'd do if a big wave of financial resource were to enter your daily life.

1. Create a simple spreadsheet or table with the following column headers: Day, Amount, and What I Bought. In the Day column, number rows 1-14.

2. In the amount column, begin row 1 with an amount of $1,000.00. For each row, double the amount listed in the Amount column. Day 2 will be $2,000, Day 3 is $4,000 and so on, until Day 14 will clock in at $8,192,000

3. Each day, your task is to spend whatever amount is in that row that day.

4. Spending rules: You must spend the ENTIRE amount in that row for that day. You cannot SAVE, INVEST or DONATE the money, nor can you use it to pay off debt.

Part of the purpose of this exercise is to get comfortable with the thought of receiving flow. When we play with these ridiculous sums of money, we are experimenting and stretching your imagination in order to expand your own ideas of what you might do with resources of that scale. I've included an example below:

DAY	AMOUNT	WHAT I PURCHASED
1	$1,000	Took my friends out to a fancy dinner and gave a very generous tip!
2	$2,000	New plants and supplies for our community garden
3	$4,000	Rent a home for a 2-week long "art sabbatical"
4	$8,000	Romantic trip to Mexico City
5	$16,000	A swimming pool!
6	$24,000	Pop-up camper for family trips
7	$32,000	Rehab our garage into a woodworking studio

PHASE 2: DESIGN

PHASE II: DESIGN

THE HOW IS IMPORTANT

Design is about intention-setting and ideation, but it is also the process of deciding on the best function and form for something. How will something be produced? Design determines what the foundation for your idea, team, or project looks like. One place to begin is by considering the ideal completed state. What would it feel like or be like to have achieved the true fulfillment of this idea? Now imagine if it felt great along the way to getting there. When you draft a blueprint of the desired outcome or future state, in addition to thinking about what you'd want the experience to feel like as you move through it, you are that much closer to realizing it.

Design is an act of balancing or braiding: weaving what you know about business needs, customer needs, environmental needs (e.g., I need transparency and confidentiality among my colleagues in terms of my own needs, but I need to be timely and on-deadline in terms of the needs of the work).

FAVORITE RESOURCES

Some of these books are incredibly practical, like those by Osterwalder, Brown, or Cameron. But some of our favorites run a bit more esoteric, and instead offer a perspective on design that asks us to expand our context, such as in Bateson and Zander's works.

- *Business Model Generation*, Alex Osterwalder
- *Theory U*, Otto Scharmer
- Emergent Strategy, adrienne maree brown

143.

- Value Proposition Design, Alexander Osterwalder
- *Conscious Evolution*, Barbara Hubbard
- *Sand Talk*, Tyson Yunkaporta
- *The Artist's Way*, Julia Cameron
- *The Art of Possibility*, Rosamund Stone Zander and Benjamin Zander
- *Small Arcs of Larger Circles*, Nora Bateson

REFLECTION QUESTIONS

Design can benefit by inviting others you trust into the inquiry. Alternative perspectives can stretch your thinking and create a stronger vision after some discussion. Consider gathering a small group to tackle a few of these reflection questions.

Is this a wild and crazy idea that won't let me rest?
What solutions light me up?
How might I design this for a team or collective?
What is this idea if I give myself full permission to scale it?
What does the project look like if it all works perfectly?
Who is this idea serving?
How is it serving my learning?
Who are my thought partners? Thought leaders?
What are the pain points you are noticing?
What would you like the story of this to be?
What can you do with a team that you cannot do alone?

AFFIRMATIONS

- I cultivate concentration and resilience
- I co-create solutions
- I am open to possibilities beyond my imagination
- I am always learning
- I am thriving / my team is thriving
- I am connected to what is most important
- I am fully living into my purpose
- I recognize in each moment I have power over my own thoughts and actions
- I always have the power to choose
- I trust in my process / in my team

The Native American Medicine Wheel, also called the Sacred Hoop, is symbolic for many Native American tribes with varying interpretations. Fundamentally, it has four quadrants that can represent: stages of life, seasons of the year, cardinal direction or the four sides of the person (physical, emotional, mental, and spiritual.

VISUALIZATION EXERCISE

As with all these visualizations, we recommend recording them by reading into your phone or laptop - or corral one of your sweet-voiced friends, colleagues or loved ones to read them into your voice memos for playback later.

Get settled, sitting upright in a chair or laying down in bed. Take 3 deep breaths and try to clear any old air in your lungs. Feel the circulation of breath. In this quiet space we are now entering, we are going to invite new, fresh perspectives to meet your hairiest problems or half-done solutions.

As you sit, imagine your feet grounded to the earth, your soles connected to the center of the core of the earth by a root of light. Imagine a tree root the color of lightning connected from the bottoms of your feet to the center of the earth. And imagine that beam

of light shining up through your legs through your trunk, up your chest into your throat and through to the crown of your head. This light starts in the earth and connects through you to the sky above. You are lit up with a vertical band of energy through your whole body. Your posture feels aligned and straight. You feel energized and present and relaxed.

And now as you settle into this new sense of relaxation, there is also a sense of connectedness. You are a part of a vast network of ideas and inspiration. Let yourself take a few deep breaths in and out. In through the nose and out through the mouth. You might even allow yourself a good sigh on the exhale.

Imagine you are seeing a map from above. This is the map of the idea or territory you are currently cultivating. Notice the landscape as you float above it: what are the features you can see from the air? Is the terrain mountainous? Do you see people moving below? You are noticing with wonder all the colors and details you hadn't realized were a part of this project or idea. You are seeing now how different routes and roads are connected, how threads and different areas come together to form a picture of the whole. You appreciate the patchwork for a moment as you stare down at the activity on the ground. Maybe you even have other insights or thoughts as you slowly descend back toward the earth.

As you touch the ground, you feel renewed and refreshed. You've gained a whole new perspective on the situation. Now you may feel a readiness. All good ideas and inspiration are ready to move through you. You have a new sense that you have everything you need for the journey of this idea or this project. What do you have gratitude for at this moment?

Take one last deep breath and come back into the room. Wiggle fingers and toes if that helps. Now slowly open your eyes.

TREASURED PRACTICES

Design applies as much to relationships as it does to a product or service. Designing how a team wants to work together, dividing responsibility, and agreeing on how to clear conflicts are just some of the elements that we can practice articulating. The most foundational of these is Designing the Alliance.

**Design the Alliance /
Creating a Team Charter**
Good for: Teams, Boards, Partnerships

A team is a set of relationships with a shared, specific purpose. Each party to the relationship has the ongoing opportunity to articulate what is important to them and what they need to feel safe, appreciated, and productive. Oftentimes, team members don't get to say out loud what is most important for them to function at their best. This practice provides an open space to share where you talk about how you want

your working relationships to be and feel within a team. In other words...

Let's talk through how to manage conflict before we actually get into a conflict!

A team charter or alliance details the expectations and behavioral norms we have that often go unspoken and misunderstood between teammates.

The practice creates:
- Sense of belonging
- Clear boundaries and norms for teams
- Shared vision and safety
- Approaching work relationships with a sense of openness and compromise
- Opportunity for team members to articulate their specific needs
- New ideas around what it means to be in partnership

Here are the steps to get started:

1. Convene a team meeting and open a fresh blank document.
2. What is the purpose or mission of your team? Agree on a 1-sentence headline
3. Have team members reflect individually and then as a group. What values are important to this team? This organization?
4. Include and draft other sections of a charter, such as:

    - A directory of members and their core roles and functions

    - Team meeting cadence and preferred platforms for communicating

    - Descriptions of back-up procedures, cross-training or other critical information

Once everyone has had an opportunity to comment on the draft agreement, the proposed edits or changes are discussed as a group. Then, everyone reads and signs the finished document.

Note: An important piece of this practice is to make sure the final artifact is available and is seen as a living document. Revisit it once a year, or whenever a norm is being reconsidered or evolving. You can use this document as a means of navigating team conversations around norms and safety.

Some other examples of specific agreements that teams have added to their team charters include:
- Confidentiality - not talking behind people's backs
- The importance of beginning and ending meetings on time
- Details on how to let team members know they don't want to be disturbed
- What pronouns folx prefer to use
- How folx prefer to receive feedback or be recognized for a job well done

Aligning on Purpose
Good for: Teams, Boards, Partnerships

Teams often jump headfirst into creating solutions. This makes sense - it's what teams are meant to do. Don't assume everyone is on the same page. Slow down at the beginning of a project and take the time as a group to define the problem together. Getting crystal clear about your shared purpose and objectives is critical to making sure the eventual solution you come up with meets the target.

When you are ready to get specific about charting a solution, this tool clarifies the purpose of a project or idea you want to undertake. When completed, this practice also illustrates the value a project will bring to you. Regardless of what type of problem you bring, here are the basic steps:

A. Define the problem(s)
What are the 2-3 core problems you are trying to solve? Use bullet points. Once you have these listed, keep asking, "Why is that a problem?" until you feel you have gotten to the very root of it. It doesn't matter if these problems are personal, professional, or a likely hybrid. Write them out in headline form. For example: "My team doesn't trust me," or "our deadline was just moved up."

B. Define the basic objective(s)
How would you know if that problem was solved? What do you want? Describe the specific goal. For example: "Increase a sense of trust in my relationships with my team by the end of the year."

C. Define the problem further or describe related problems. For example: "Since our team has gone remote, it is difficult to feel a sense of cohesion in the team."

D. Define any other objectives that arise which relate. For example: "More informal time communicating with my colleagues."

E. Create a Concept
The concept is a vision of the actual solution that you want to implement in order to solve the original problem. It can consist of a list of high-level characteristics of a solution.
What do you need to build in order to truly meet these objectives? Look closely at the relationship between the original problem and the objectives you have written. From those pieces, a potential solution can emerge. What product or concept can address the issues you've set forth?

**PHASE 3:
ENACT**

PHASE III: ENACT

MANAGING THE "DOING" ENERGY

We see the image of a conductor tapping their baton against the podium, and the music that immediately follows and swells...

Enact is the setting-into-motion of the careful intentions and designs that you (and your team or organization) made into a commitment and a plan. To enact with a conscious awareness and a spirit of mindfulness is crucial during uncertain times.

FAVORITE RESOURCES

Gallup StrengthsFinder
Enneagram Test
Astrology! (for fun)
Radical Candor, Kim Scott
Five Dysfunctions of a Team, Patrick Lencioni
How We Show Up, Mia Birdsong
Insight, Tasha Eurich

REFLECTION QUESTIONS

- What kind of pacing or energy do I want to bring into this project?
- What does it mean for me to "finish strong?"
- What do I expect of myself?
- How would I like myself / my team to perform?
- What can we do together that we cannot do alone?
- What is emerging?
- What feels urgent now?
- Where in my body do I feel a sense of readiness to start?
- Where do I feel ease and flow?
- What brings me energy?

AFFIRMATIONS

- We are all in this together I move things forward, I am a catalyst for change
- May I continue to adapt and grow
- May this project fulfill its highest purpose
- I am a master coordinator
- May all my communications be smooth and effective
- We have everything we need

- I am aligned with my purpose
- As within, so without (from the Hermetic Corpus, an expression of the interconnectedness of all things).

VISUALIZATION EXERCISE

As with all these visualizations, we recommend recording them by reading into your phone or laptop -- or corral one of your sweet-voiced friends, colleagues or loved ones to read them into your voice memos for playback later.

To start this visualization, please sit comfortably. Close your eyes. Take 1-2 deep breaths. Try to sit with your back and neck straight but relaxed. Allow yourself to become more relaxed with every breath you take as your breath slows down.

Notice how each breath affects your body. With each inhale deeper into your chest and belly, drawing the energy from the whole world, allowing the energy to circulate through your being and back into the universe.

As you continue to focus on your breath, visualize yourself at the top of a downwards-facing staircase just in front of you. It's a bright and welcoming staircase that leads you down to a deeper part of your imagination. We're going to step down; with each breath we'll go deeper and deeper into your place of dreaming. This part of you connects to the universe; to that which is 'All That Is'.

Ten steps lead downward. Just allow yourself to go slowly down one step at a time, allowing your body to relax everywhere and allow the energy to circulate freely in your body. As you step down another step and another, find that your muscles in the

head begin to relax. Your jaw relaxes, your forehead relaxes, even the muscles of the eyeballs relax as do the muscles of the eyelids, your neck, the muscles of the shoulders, the back... everything starts relaxing. The tongue doesn't touch the roof of the mouth. Everything is becoming heavier, settling down as we're going down towards the core of your being.

When we reach the bottom step, allow yourself to feel the consciousness expanding. Feel yourself as if floating in the universe. Allow your thoughts and worries to dissolve and disappear, just for now, just for today.

As you step off the last step, you notice it opens out onto a limitless field of flowers. The air is fragrant and mild. You are surrounded by your favorite flowers (or plants), and they are gently swaying in the breeze. In this sunny place, you bend down to get a closer look at one of the stems. You

lean down almost as if your face is ground-level. You notice the smallest details - the little hairs or thorns on the stems, the texture of the petals perhaps, maybe you see a small ladybug clinging to a leaf. You take a moment to appreciate the nuance and the perfection of each small aspect of it.

You select one stem and then you stand back up, holding the flower or plant up to the sun.
You see it as you hold it up against the sky and notice the contrast of it against the bright blue. You notice the perfect outline of the plant in the sunlight. You hold the flower in such a way that you can see it against the backdrop of thousands of other flowers stretching out beyond the horizon. In this moment you see both the detail and the big picture. Take a breath here and just be with that picture in your mind.

Now it is time to go back to your regular daily life

for now. And so you are turning around and slowly walking back toward the stairs you arrived from. There is a doorway and you move through the threshold, stepping up onto the stairway and begin to ascend the 10 slow steps up to the very top. And as you do this, you bring your attention back to your slow and steady breathing. Inhales and exhales.

TREASURED PRACTICES

Gifts Process
Good for: Self, Teams
Creates: Reconnection to self and your unique value, recognition among team members, trust

Part I. Grab your journal and answer the following questions:

1. Think of a time when you gave of yourself completely and passionately to a project, event, job, relationship, or other activity. Something you found especially fulfilling. What unique attributes did you bring to that? What was unique about the way you gave of yourself to the person, group, or project?

2. What do you think are your top 3 strengths? (Remember these are more like attributes, traits, gifts, rather than skills you have mastered. These are things that are innate to you)
3. What would the people who know you best in the world say are your top 3 strengths?

Part II. Enlist those who know you best, who really see you: Invite 4-5 very close friends or confidantes and ask them to comment on the following questions:

1. How do they experience you?
2. What are their impressions of your unique gifts?
3. What do they appreciate most about you?

Have them email you back their responses. What you see mirrored back to you is a reflection of your special genius and what the people who know you best appreciate the most about who you are. The results are insightful and expand our perceptions of ourselves.

Tip for Teams: If you have a close-knit team, you could randomly assign colleagues to one another to fill out the questionnaire on one another's behalf.

Note: Refrain from asking or eliciting critical feedback. e.g., don't ask for comments on weaknesses. That isn't the point of this particular exercise, and may activate your inner critic voice/gremlin.

TEAM PRACTICES to ENACT

In TEAM PRACTICES, we introduce five core exercises that, when done with some consistency, transform the ways in which we and our teams

157.

operate. Some of the activities are tuned to the individual while others are meant to be done in a group. In our own work lives, we have found these exercises to be incredibly fruitful and transformative -- changing the dynamics of the team for the better, and growing a sense of closeness and alignment which benefits overall communications and work product. As with everything, what you pay attention to, grows. So as we focus some explicit attention on the matrix of relationships that make up our teams, we will see resulting positive shifts in how the team feels and does its work together.

Using these practices doesn't have to be rigid, but when ritualized or habitualized in your team, they become a restorative and generative part of its operating system. The practices build emotional intelligence and resilience. We can anticipate and move forward together, past any initial

awkwardness, discomfort, or embarrassment of being real and vulnerable with our colleagues. What these exercises yield is a growing sense of trust, candor, and compassion for one another. This is a game changer. Having an increased spirit of generosity and empathy for each other reduces friction during the regular day-to-day deadlines, tasks and tensions that can form a "waxy build-up" inside and among the relationships on our teams.

These practices work on the HOW of our work together, rather than the WHAT. Initiating a habit like a daily bow to one another, for example, can show respect, thankfulness, and presence. In these moments, notice the effort we invest into our relationships within the team. Work gets done, deals get made, and projects are completed based on the health, depth, and quality of the relationships in and among our teams. All of these exercises are designed to strengthen and reinforce the social fabric and quality of your relationships with your colleagues.

These practices are in a specific sequence. Begin by addressing your own needs, and then move into the group practices.

1. Nourish List
2. Daily Gratitude
3. Daily Standup
4. Japanese Chorei
5. Bowing 101
6. Breakdowns & Breakthroughs

1. NOURISH LIST

Creates: Reconnection to self and self-care, empathy and self-compassion

If you are noticing that you are not showing up in conversations authentically, that can be feedback that you haven't been nurturing yourself; that your battery is low or there is an energy deficit. Self-care is in order. Sometimes I feel this way when I recognize the needs of others over my own (this is very common for parents). If I recognize my own needs first, I can show up more fully, more consciously, and kick ass in the world without burning out. So spend a little time reflecting on the practices, activities, rituals that fill you back up. What are the things that nurture you? What can you happily lose yourself in?

Make a list of at least 10 things / activities that nourish you (e.g. running, singing, yoga, painting, etc.) How might you incorporate any one of those more fully into your daily life?

159.

2. DAILY GRATITUDE
Creates: Appreciation, compassion, generosity, more gratitude

Every morning set aside 5 minutes for this just upon waking. Keep a journal or notepad next to the bed. Write down five things that you are grateful for that immediately come to mind. (Avoid making the list on your phone, as you are likely to then over engage with your phone.) The team version of this is just a daily standup that allows each colleague to share a couple things they were grateful for. It's best to do it early in the workday, as a way to ground the team in appreciation as the day begins.

Extra credit: Contemplate why you are thankful for them, or how they made you feel.
Next to each thing you are grateful for, take a sentence to answer "Why did this happen?"

3. THE DAILY STANDUP
Creates: Synchronicity, appreciation, understanding, grounding toward common goal

The daily standup is a central practice that any agile team lives by. It's called standup because the meeting must always be brief enough to stand through, to think about efficiency, interconnectedness and strategy together for 10-15 minutes every morning as your workday begins. During the years I managed teams of software engineers, the standup became a series of brief rituals that united us as a team and refocused us in the same direction. It was the single most useful communication device in all of the best teams I've worked on. And because it was held in a circle, there was no sense of hierarchy in the moments where communication counted the most.

4. JAPANESE CHOREI
Creates: Positivity, championing openness and sharing, honoring the team

The daily stand up originated from the chorei (chor-rei), a traditional cornerstone of Japanese business. It's an important way to feel connected to everyone and its attendance is mandatory. It's a practice that helps everyone feel motivated to share and participate. What makes the Japanese stand-up a bit different is the inclusion of "put-ups" where a new team member enjoys shout-outs by their team members. What's more important is that the chorei isn't a share-out but rooted in positivity. You and your teams can make this short 10-15 min your own, but make sure it's grounded in belonging and keeping your team inspired and motivated.

5. BOWING 101
Creates: Respect, grounding

This practice is the simple act of bowing to your colleagues before a meeting begins. It can initially be uncomfortable to try this out, but the results are wonderful. Before you take your seats at the meeting, stand around the table (in a circle ideally). Take a pause together and bow toward the center of the circle. Then, start your meeting as you normally would. A former mentor explained the power of a team bowing to one another as they began common work: as we move our heads down toward the center of the circle, we send our best thoughts, intentions, and intellect, toward the central common purpose of the project we are on. At first the team grumbled about it, but after a while it became a real sign of respect and a moment of pause so that we could be in the present moment together and start the meeting off on a solid note.

6. BREAKDOWNS & BREAKTHROUGHS

Creates: Trust. Sharing mistakes and difficulties can build resilience, the ability to pivot and change POV in the moment, and improvise.

This is a powerful weekly exercise to do with a team, but I also do it for myself as a regular practice in my writing. It gives your colleagues a ton of context about one another and creates a lot of compassion. Doing this regularly can uncover the assumptions and stories that we create about ourselves and one another without even knowing. Breakthroughs are nuggets of learning, eurekas, moments of clarity or jumps in understanding. Breakdowns denote some way in which the colleague has changed.

If you are in a group, stand in a circle and go clockwise with each person taking a turn (2 minutes max per person)
Each person takes a turn to share a challenge (or a breakdown) that they have had recently at work. Breakdowns can happen within the context of a communication, discovering misalignment in the context of a project, or a lack of clarity around a task.
Next, they then share something they have learned (or breakthrough) from the challenge thus far.

Extra credit: Volunteer to go first. As a leader, it is a powerful gesture since this exercise can be exposing and requires vulnerability.

RITUAL

Rituals celebrate the milestones of life. They build social fabric and add deeper meaning to the everyday routines that make up our life. Birthday candle wishes, weddings, and even the regular nightly bedtime stories are examples of rituals that acknowledge connection and give meaning to time. Ritual draws us into the moment and captures our attention, tuning us to the subtle energies all around.

Rituals allow us a tangible way to notice and celebrate what is meaningful. They set an intention to honor the everyday gifts we receive from nature, one another, and Spirit. Your rituals, whether through meditation, forging an altar space, or journaling, can be set with the most basic intention of giving something your precious attention and time.

Rituals, by calling in and focusing on connections of all kinds, can give comfort and clarity during times of uncertainty and confusion. Yes, even at work, secular rituals can be incorporated into your management of teams. For example, to close out a project with a retrospective discussion with your team in circle. Here are some questions and examples to help you think through the building blocks of a ritual.

Who is this for?	What is the Intention/purpose?	What is the Context? These are prompts or milestones or moments to commemorate	How the process goes the flow or script of it - (this is how you actually conduct the ritual)	What is the cadence of this ritual?
Individual	Slow down / ground to make a decision	Delivering a product	Freewriting - 15 min	Daily
1/1	Calm down	Hiring someone new	Gratitude practice - list of 10 items	Weekly
Team or Group	Gain clarity, clarify thinking	Letting go of someone or someone departing	Sitting in circle	Monthly
Org-wide/ whole system	Feeling overwhelmed or chaotic and need to get grounded	New leader starting	"Make the peace" staring at candle	Quarterly
Everyone (global) or all living beings	Commit to a goal	Closing a project	Dyad walk (walking conversation and reflection)	As needed (ad hoc) as the community asks for it - sense into it
Leaders	Celebrate the end of something	Launching a new project	Dance party	Annually
Customers or specific community	Celebrate the beginning of something	Calendar milestone like close of fiscal year or company anniversary	Silent meditation - 15 min	One-off
	Reassurance and comfort		Create "Nourish List" or inventory of activities that recharge your battery (e.g. hiking)	

Adding sacred acts back into the daily:

- Morning pages (*The Artist's Way*)
- Journaling
- Morning, evening, mid-day 5-10 minute meditation breaks
- Tea or coffee ceremonies throughout the day
- 1-2 minute silence to open a group meeting (better yet, in between virtual calls)
- Nourishment / quiet eating (away from phones and distractions)
- Quiet walks, no media, walking meditation
- Create an altar
- Prayer
- Ceremonies

JOURNALING

A daily gratitude journal where you reflect nightly on what you are grateful for, during that day's activities, will transform your outlook and vibration within a week.

ALTARS

Whether indoor or outdoor, a space to meditate or even a small table with a cloth over it, can be adorned with the important sacred items that you want to bring forth. A picture of your ancestors, incense, seashells, items found in nature, symbolic tokens, flowers, crystals -- whatever you choose as a dedication. The altar reminds you to make time for quiet and reflection. Choose items that connect you to something bigger than yourself.

MEDITATION

There are so many forms of it! But if there is a takeaway we want this book to leave for you, it's about getting quiet. We've been asked (accused, even), "Are you meditating or asleep?," or "Are you really meditating because it seems like you are asleep." We've varied our meditations in the many ways but it can be:

- Guided meditation (YouTube videos, Spotify playlists, so many apps)

- Walking meditation (A short 5 to 10 minute walk even in your house where you, without any devices or media, thoughtfully pace and feel the earth and steps you take.)

- Incense burning (Lighting a favorite incense stick, gazing into it, and watching the smoke dissipate

Enjoy the exploration of meditation! From sitting up with your eyes open, to laying flat on your

back, there are so many practices and so many forms. Choose what is best for you and integrate it into your daily practice.

SOLSTICE AND EQUINOX FIRE CEREMONIES

A favorite ceremony to do with a group of loved friends or family is to gather together on the solstices and/or equinoxes for a "burning ceremony" around a fire pit or bonfire.

This can be as long or as simple as you'd like this to be:

1. Open the ceremony with calling in your divinity of choice: ancestors, spirits, or the love that brings everyone together that day/evening.

2. Invite each person to take 3 pieces of paper and create a list of the following using ink, not pencil:

- a) Purge and Release: what do you want to release from your life? Situation? Avoid naming names, but do name the dynamic (e.g. not your mother-in-law's name v. her complaining texts).
- b) Gratitude: Whatcha grateful for? Good to name names here!
- c) Manifestation: All your hopes and dreams.

3. Safely start your fire (if you haven't already) and begin by asking the Universe to purge the things they've listed on the first slip of paper. Everyone takes one final look and says a private word of gratitude for that list and the lessons learned. Then everyone puts JUST that list into the fire.

4. Once completed, move onto the Gratitude list in the same fashion, and when everyone has put that list into the fire, then repeat the same with the Manifestation.
Note: Also fun to take a picture of the lists (not the purge one) to see what comes true!

5. Close the ceremony with any final words and sit back as the Universe listens to your prayers.

Notes: This almost always works but be careful as it can all happen at once! One thing to be clear about: trust in divine timing. If you are asking for a new job, the perfect one will present itself when it's the right time. Ask for the dream to be fulfilled when you are ready to receive it. Manifest the underlying feeling and desire. e.g. While it's OK to be specific about the Porsche, it's almost better to name the desire of a luxury car, that drives fast and gives you the feeling of abundance, for example. And, no one needs to share what they've written down, but sometimes it's helpful to shout out a collective dream, e.g. purge my student loan debt, or manifest justice!

"THEMES" FOR YOUR CEREMONY

Winter Solstice: As the darkest day of the year, this ceremony is wonderful to celebrate and purge the "darkness" of the year. It's a favorite because the winter also represents hibernation and the start of an introspective time.

Spring Equinox: Spring is a great time to give an extra focus on manifestation and what you want to bring into the year.

Summer Solstice: The shortest day of the year, full of sun and brightness, it's a great ceremony to emphasize manifestation and abundance.

Fall Equinox: Representative of the harvest, it's great to focus on gratitude here before entering the winter.

In the democracy originally designed by many First Nations, indigenous peoples from all over the world honored guidance from elders. There were fewer ruling positions, but elders provided guidance based on their experience and judgment. This collective wisdom was rooted in the greatest good and balance for all, and harmony with nature, honoring that we are visitors in these short times of our lives.

PHASE 4:
ALLOW

PHASE IV: ALLOW

THE ART OF LETTING GO

So many of our problems and challenges can be seen through a lens of our own resistance to the thing. The exercises in this section have to do with noticing our crankiness or attachments, moving stuck energy, and staying open to possibility. Allowing could mean stepping back from our controlling habits and giving our team some breathing room. Or it could mean giving ourselves permission to dream bigger. The idea is to release what binds us or keeps us down.

FAVORITE RESOURCES

The Self-Aware Universe, Amit Goswani
7 Habits of Highly Effective People, Stephen Covey
Tao de Ching, Stephen Mitchell translation/edition
Courage to Change (al-anon)
Holding Space, Heather Plett
Perseverance, Margaret J. Wheatley
Finding Our Way podcast with Prentis Hemphill
Braiding Sweetgrass, Robin Wall Kimmerer
We Will Not Cancel Us, adrienne maree brown

REFLECTION QUESTIONS

- What might I be resisting?
- What am I holding on to that no longer serves?
- What feels stuck?
- Where are the bright spots?
- Think back to a time when you recognize your value. What were the circumstances?
- Where in my body do I feel resistance?

- Where in my body do I feel relaxed?
- What would feel good right now?
- What would my future self have to say about this scenario?
- What help do I need now?
- How am I open to new ways of being and doing?
- Where do I see new connections?

AFFIRMATIONS

- My work is in flow
- I am grounded in my purpose
- Other people's opinions of me are none of my business
- My actions are aligned with my authentic self
- My intentions are clear and true
- I own my value
- My internal guidance system is strong
- I cultivate resilience and perseverance
- I keep my eyes on the horizon
- I allow all good things to flow to me
- I allow love to surround me

VISUALIZATION

This is a very simple grounding exercise by Eckhart Tolle, designed to help us get in touch with our inner sense of aliveness.

Close your eyes and hold out one hand.
Allow yourself to feel your hand with your other hand. Then move your hands apart.
Now ask yourself: without touching anything, without moving your hand again, and without looking at your hand, how can you know that your hand is still there? If you pay attention, you realize that you can feel the inside of your hand, a subtle sense of warmth or tingling.
Keeping your eyes closed, now move your attention slowly to the rest of your body and feel that sense of warmth/tingling throughout. As you notice each place, perhaps imagine a wave of color flowing over the places you notice warmth and aliveness.

Add progressively more and more parts of your body until you can feel that sense of aliveness and see yourself covered in color, through every single cell.

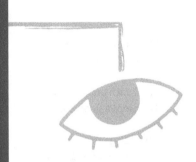

TREASURED PRACTICES

IMPROVISATION
Activities that center on allow or allowing are often tied to emergence. Emergence is very present when doing improvisation. In an adaptation of the standard improv exercise Story-Story, a team or group sits or stands in a circle. A facilitator or host stands in the middle and gives a setting for the story. She then points to a person in the circle and they begin telling a story. After the first storyteller has described the beginning of the story, the facilitator selects another person. The story continues on; the new person picks up from the last word and continues the narrative.

Everyone should get several turns to add to the story. Usually the host suggests when the story comes to a conclusion; however, more in-sync groups will be able to conclude their story on their own. To adapt this to a business-setting, the prompt for the start of the story could be specifically tuned to a business challenge or narrative that is relevant to the team at the time, for example "Once upon a time, we had the greatest season our department had ever known..." This exercise could support the development of rich user stories as leaders provide prompts and allow their teams to daydream and brainstorm how the good story might unfold.

STREAM & DREAM

A magical morning practice that focuses your desires, this daily exercise is about making a ritual of articulating your daydreams and goals, allowing them to become clear and tangible.

First thing in the morning, open the Voice Memo or a recording app on your phone. Start recording!

2 MIN - Talk about what you are grateful for, stream of consciousness style. Feel the gratitude flow in your body, let it put a smile on your face.

2 MIN - Talk about your daily desires as if they've already happened, "Today felt delicious because..." Go into details. Talk about the entire day from start to finish in the past tense.

2 MIN - Talk about your future desires as if they've already happened. "It feels great to have traveled to Fiji!" Talk about your career, love, health, creativity whatever is of value to you.

Accountability FTW: Send this recording to someone who truly supports you. They can listen and send one back. We've tried this with circles of peers, and it has been a game-changer to help envision a successful day.

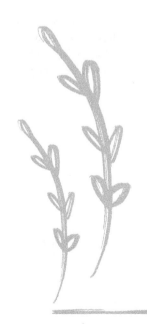

"RELEASE" LIST

Make a list, handwritten is preferred, of all the things (about yourself, about your life) that you want to release. Here are some common examples from our lists: self-doubt, fear, guilt, you get the idea. You can be general or specific, just be authentic.

Go on writing the list for 2 or 3 minutes. Stop whenever it doesn't flow out easily anymore (that's a good tip for any of these exercises).

The final step is to burn (preferred) or shred (more office-friendly) the list. Release and recycle that shiz.

SITTING WITH THE TROUBLE

In this exercise, we practice allowing difficulty. We practice being at peace with the hard things in work and life. We practice not resisting these things. We practice being with imperfect circumstances; cultivating our resilience. The most challenging part about troubles is that we often carry them without seeing them. When we face them, it is never as scary as we predicted. It can be such a liberating experience to realize we are bigger than that, we are more than just our troubles.

1. Start with 2 minutes of sitting still in silence, no distractions. Anchor yourself in your breath.

2. Ask yourself: What does trouble mean to you? (e.g., being with difficulty, discomfort, challenge) Bring to mind a trouble you see in your life right now: different troubles have a different weight on you.

3. Pick a medium-sized trouble. How does it feel in your body? Color or texture? Does it make your heart beat faster? Does it have a smell?

4. Give yourself 10-15 minutes to journal, doodle, draw or create some type of artifact related to this trouble or the feelings coming up around it.

5. To finish the practice, you can burn your trouble artifact or even make it part of a shrine to remind you of your patience and growth in this area. (Notice the intention of however you choose to dispose of or keep it, is it a reminder of the process to you and you want to preserve it or enshrine it? is it something you want to purge and therefore burn or purge it, etc.?

Note: This is an exercise that can be done solo or in a team. It helps to have a guide.

LEADERSHIP

The Wheel helps us to model being a leader who centers reflection, vulnerability, and transparency. Successful leaders of the in-between walk their talk. Integrity is top of mind, and means taking a service mindset toward teams and organizations. To have a service mindset means beginning with the aim of earning authority rather than flexing it. These leaders understand the health and wellbeing of their teams is in direct relationship to the success of the whole endeavor. The system is interdependent; we are all in this together. This leader commits to not only steering the ship, but developing a culture of care and core practices so that the whole ecosystem thrives.

If you are in a role of managing, building, or developing teams, we invite you to observe your daily management practices. How do you stay in close touch with your team? When do you feel most confident in your leadership? Your position is critical because as the lead you are also caretaker, helper and change agent. Here are a few exercises we use with our teams:

Weekly one-on-one check in
The weekly check in is a must. It can be very quick, but important for what we call "sense-making" to be helpful and on the same page with each of your teammates. Here are the core two things to discuss:

- Priorities
- How can we support one another

How can I check in EVERY week with someone? First, take opportunities to make your organization aware of the time it takes to manage a team. Second, notice your own limits. If you feel tapped out after 15 direct report check-ins and you haven't yet gotten to your own work, that is an indication that you've surpassed the maximum number of people you should manage.

Problem Solving Inquiry
Instead of telling the team 'figure it out,' (or worse, doing the work yourself) the following prompts can help uncover what someone is actually asking for:
- Let's walk through your thought process
- What are our options?
- What can I help with?
- What's the desired outcome? What do we want to have happen?
- What resources are available to help with this?

Modeling behavior
Your team is looking to you to provide information and feedback directly and quickly. You (and your style) are the main influence on your team. Notice how you show up. Are you scattered? Are you grounded? Are you constantly connecting dots, attempting to decipher who needs what information and when? There are ways to orchestrate without creating additional chaos or overwhelm. Your vibe and tone set the culture. Build rapport by checking in as a group at least twice a week:

1. Begin and close the week with intentions. Have you completed what you set out to do?

2. Has this week felt good? Where have we seen support and appreciation?

3. What feedback or takeaways should we all keep in mind?

GUIDEBOOK TO ME (inspired by Cassie Robinson)

We often learn about one another through the act of working together. We build and create things together, run projects together, but many times our preferences go unsaid. Think of this exercise as a great check-in for your colleagues to get a deeper look at one another's needs and styles when it comes to work. As Robinson describes, "There should be a caveat that this [exercise] is done knowing that not all your needs and preferences can be met, but there is still value in making them explicit for those you work with."[11]

My archetype…(name someone - a fictional character or an IRL person you admire)

My ideal office environment…

My peak times for work are…

The best ways or platforms to communicate with me…

How to tell me I'm doing a good job…

Things I need…

My quirks or struggles…

Things I go wild for…

Something my oldest friend would tell you about me…

[11] Robinson, Cassie. "A user manual for me," *Medium*. https://cassierobinson.medium.com/a-user-manual-for-me-d3a851fbc694. August 26, 2017.

STAYING IN MOTION

First, gratitude. Thank you for being on this journey with us. Thank you for your delicious curiosity. This inquiry of ours into how work will be different is constantly shifting. This is part of the nature of the in-between. As we write to you from the past, we are concentrating on the present moment: getting this book into your hands so that you can begin experimenting with a more spiritual and deeper perspective on work and teams.

Our Highest Hope
We see workplaces where everyone is connected to their purpose. We see deeper bonds and trust between colleagues and among leaders and their teams. We see people investing in new ways of communicating and prioritizing relationships. Practices and messages like the ones in this book continue to flourish and evolve and take root across the globe.

Lastly, while the In-Between has focused on transformation for work and leadership, as well as individual healing, it's not lost on us that most of our humanity is simply surviving and enduring our changing, and challenging times. Basic needs like food on the table and a roof over heads will always trump considerations for transformation. Give where you can to heal the collective.

If you'd like help designing exercises and experiments specifically for your organization, or would just like to chat about the state of "work" and the in-between, you can contact us at hello@theinbetween.world

TALK TO US:
We are excited to work with teams and organizations who are ready to change. Would you like to bring the In-Between to your teams? We would love to support your personal or organization's growth through:

- Facilitation - personal and team
- Retreat and Strategy Session Design
- Workshops and team building using sociocracy, liberating structures, art of hosting
- Start-up / emerging organizations
- Finance, Strategy and Operations
- Diversity, Equity, Inclusion and Belonging
- Business design
- Organizational Development

Here's how you can engage with us: please visit www.inbetween.world or email hello@theinbetween.world.

Keep up all the amazing introspection and innovation. We can't wait to hear your stories. Become a part of our community of ideators and at the-in-between.world.

CPSIA information can be obtained
at www.ICGtesting.com
Printed in the USA
BVHW051657271222
655065BV00012B/336